Essential JSP™ for
Web Professionals

ISBN 0-13-064941-4

9 780130 649416

90000

- *Essential CSS & DHTML for Web Professionals, Second Edition*
  Dan Livingston

- *Essential JSP™ for Web Professionals*
  Damon Hougland and Aaron Tavistock

- *Essential WAP for Web Professionals*
  Damon Hougland and Khurram Zafar

- *Essential GIMP for Web Professionals*
  Michael Hammel

- *Essential ColdFusion 4.5 for Web Professionals*
  Micah Brown and Mike Fredrick

- *Essential Design for Web Professionals*
  Charles Lyons

- *Essential Flash™ 5 for Web Professionals*
  Lynn Kyle

- *Essential Flash™ 4 for Web Professionals*
  Lynn Kyle

- *Essential ASP for Web Professionals*
  Elijah Lovejoy

- *Essential PHP for Web Professionals*
  Christopher Cosentino

- *Essential JavaScript™ for Web Professionals*
  Dan Barrett, Dan Livingston, and Micah Brown

- *Essential Perl 5 for Web Professionals*
  Micah Brown, Chris Bellow, and Dan Livingston

- *Essential Photoshop® 5 for Web Professionals*
  Brad Eigen, Dan Livingston, and Micah Brown

Essential JSP™ for Web Professionals

Damon Hougland
Aaron Tavistock

Prentice Hall PTR
Upper Saddle River, NJ 07458
www.phptr.com

Library of Congress Cataloging-in-Publication Data

Hougland, Damon.
   Essential JSP for Web professionals/Damon Hougland and Aaron Tavistock.
    p.cm.—(The Prentice Hall essential Web professionals series)
   ISBN 0-13-064941-4
    1. Java (Computer program language) 2. JavaServer pages. 3. Web servers. I.
Hougland, Damon. II. Title. III. Series.

QA76.73.J38T38 2001
005.7'2--dc21

2001033133

Editorial/Production Supervisor: Donna Cullen-Dolce
Acquisitions Editor: Karen McLean
Marketing Manager: Dan DePasquale
Manufacturing Manager: Alexis R. Heydt
Cover Design: DesignSource
Interior Design Director: Gail Cocker-Bogusz
Series Design: Patti Guerrieri

© 2002 Prentice Hall PTR
Prentice-Hall, Inc.
Upper Saddle River, NJ 07458

Prentice Hall books are widely used by corporations and government agencies for training, marketing, and resale.

The publisher offers discounts on this book when ordered in bulk quantities. For more information, contact: Corporate Sales Department, Phone: 800-382-3419; Fax: 201-236-7141; E-mail: corpsales@prenhall.com; or write: Prentice Hall PTR, Corp. Sales Dept., One Lake Street, Upper Saddle River, NJ 07458.

Printed in the United States of America

10 9 8 7 6 5 4 3 2 1

ISBN 0-13-064941-4

Pearson Education LTD.
Pearson Education Australia PTY, Limited
Pearson Education Singapore, Pte. Ltd.
Pearson Education North Asia Ltd.
Pearson Education Canada, Ltd.
Pearson Educación de Mexico, S.A. de C.V.
Pearson Education—Japan
Pearson Education Malaysia, Pte. Ltd.
Pearson Education, Upper Saddle River, New Jersey

Dedication

From Damon

I dedicate all of my efforts in creating this book to my grandfather Jack Charles Wells. You are my real mentor. Your guidance, understanding, and the example you set with the integrity and honor with which you live your life have always guided me on the right path. Thank you, Papa. This one's for you.

Aaron, thanks for being my co-author. You are a long and true friend. Writing a book is one of the most difficult things I have attempted; working with you has made a difficult task bearable. Your friendship and support helped me all the way.

From Aaron

This book is dedicated to the most important person in my life, my daughter, Zella Arden Tavistock-Thaman. You are the most wonderful little girl in the world, always full of curiosity, beauty, and glee. Words cannot do justice to how much I love you.

Raquella thank you for being such a spectacular mother and kind nurturer for our beautiful baby. In the chaotic environment that I spin around myself, you are the stabilizing force that keeps me from tipping over.

For my parents, Daniel and Marjie, thank you for being such great supporters and benefactors of the entire clan. Thanks to all of my sisters; Rachel, Anna, Katie, and Amy—you are each different in many ways but we all share more similarities than differences.

Of course, I have to give very significant thanks to my co-author, Damon Hougland. We've been through a lot—working together, writing software, running businesses, and authoring books. This second book could never have happened without his drive to get it done.

Thank you, everyone.

Contents

Foreword

Back in early 90s (the good ol' days) during the birth of client server, I actually had a purpose as a technical architect. Back then, languages changed almost daily as competing technologies preached the wonders of their particular syntax. Simultaneously, industry analysts and futurists were constantly telling software development professionals that CASE tools would soon make us all obsolete.

Well here we are in 2001. A new generation of software development professionals has emerged—professionals who are by no means obsolete but are instead an integral part of any business enterprise. The Internet has invaded every part of life as we know it, and while the dot.com craze has finally ended, corporations of all sizes are rushing to "Web-enable" their enterprise. Development languages have stabilized as well. No longer do people debate the importance of object-oriented programming, cross platform portability, open systems, etc.; these issues are assumed resolved.

Much of this standardization on Web-based architectures and object-based development can be tied directly to the advent of the Java programming language. JavaServer Pages and Java Servlets based on this language have allowed software development professionals to design complex, enterprise-wide applications that can run on any platform, in any environment (Web, client server, stand-alone) without any rewrite. Also issues of scalability and extensibility that used to plague development professionals in the past are solved though JSP's object-oriented architecture.

Damon Hougland is my colleague at eFORCE, Inc. At eFORCE, we pride ourselves in the expertise we bring to our clients in the truly transformational technologies, including JSP, that help them achieve their goals. Damon works as a technical leader to help our clients refine their objectives and define practical solutions that meet their market goals, technology, and budget constraints. *Essential JSP for Web Professionals* is based on years of Damon's practical experience, coupled with his solid theoretical knowledge. This unparalleled combination makes for a unique book.

Essential JSP for Web Professionals covers all the basic concepts involved in JSP programming and has a repertoire of practical application examples for the software development professional. Back in the good ol' days when I was a developer, I searched for books like *Essential JSP* to provide me with real-world examples to assist me in coming up the learning curve on a technology. Damon's practical examples are written by a developer for a developer. I am confident that you will find them very helpful.

Damon's straightforward approach to teaching critical concepts of JSP is refreshing. He also provides the rigor and critical architecture insight required to develop robust enterprise-wide solutions. I believe you will find this book valuable not only to learn JSP for the first time, but you will use it time and time again as a reference to assist you through your JSP development endeavors.

I hope you enjoy *Essential JSP for Web Professionals* as much as I did.

Wayne L. Flake
Regional Vice President
EFORCE, Inc.

Acknowledgments

Without help from several different people this book would have never happened. Their guidance through the entire process kept us on track and focused.

Our editor, Karen McLean, supported us throughout the entire project, patiently answering our questions and guiding us onto the right path. Additionally our production editor, Donna Cullen-Dolce, did a fabulous job of shaping our manuscript into the finished form you see today.

Thanks also goes to John Hitchcock, Loren Niespolo, and Robin Kemkes, who helped us create the professional and descriptive images used throughout the book.

Thanks goes to Wayne Flake, who loaned his insight and perspective to create the poignant foreword that begins this book.

Finally, we would also like to thank the entire JSP community. Countless individuals have put in hundreds of hours to grow and evolve JSP into a powerful tool for business today. The JSP and open source community is a model for building best of breed technologies, and it serves as a lighthouse for future efforts.

About the Authors

DAMON HOUGLAND is the author of *Core JSP™* and *Essential JSP™ for Web Professionals* from Prentice Hall/PTR. He is a Senior Director of Operations for eFORCE, Inc., where he designs and architects Java enterprise applications. Damon is in charge of leading project operations and delivery for wireless and eBusiness integration projects in the Central region. He manages customer and key partner relationships and helps define the technologies and methodologies utilized in the successful execution of eFORCE projects.

Previously, Damon led the Web application infrastructure team at Lawrence Berkeley National Laboratory, which specialized in reporting scientific data through Web-enabled databases and applications. He has worked in system integration and system administration at companies such as Sun Microsystems, Palm Computing, and Motorola during the last nine years.

AARON TAVISTOCK is the co-author of *Core JSP™* from Prentice Hall/PTR. He has over a decade of experience with application development and UNIX systems. During this time, he has worked as a UNIX systems administrator, software engineer, and technical architect.

Aaron is currently the Director of Engineering at ZipRealty, the nation's largest online real estate brokerage. His team has created a J2EE-based customer relationship and transaction management platform that is leading the technology revolution in real estate.

1 An Overview of JSP

While JavaServer Pages™ (JSP) is still a somewhat new technology, the speed at which it is becoming a standard for creating enterprise-class Web applications is amazing. While Java technology has been slowly gaining ground in client/server and standalone applications, with both JSP and Java servlets, Java has become the major platform for large-scale eBusiness applications.

◆ 1.1 Server-Side Scripting and Servlets

To better understand why JSP has risen so fast in the realm of Web application development, it is best to have a brief introduction to server-side scripting languages and Java servlets.

1.1.1 Server-Side Scripting Solutions

There are several common scripting solutions to create Web applications. These are scripts that are run on the server before the page is sent to the user.

Netscape's server-side scripting solution is called Server-Side JavaScript (SSJS). In SSJS, JavaScript is executed on the server to modify HTML pages. In SSJS, scripts are precompiled to improve server performance. SSJS is available on several different versions of Netscape Web servers. To learn more about SSJS, go to: *http://developer.netscape.com/tech/javascript/ssjs/ssjs.html.*

Microsoft servers offer Active Server Pages (ASP). ASP is very similar to JSP. ASP allows developers to embed VBScript or JScript code directly into a Web page. ASP has to be compiled every time it is run, mirroring one of the major drawbacks of Common Gateway Interface (CGI) scripts. ASP is available to developers running Microsoft's Internet Information Server 3.0 or above.

By far, the biggest drawback of the major scripting solutions is their proprietary nature. All of the solutions discussed are dependent on either certain Web servers or specific vendors.

1.1.2 Java Servlets

Java servlets are a powerful alternative to CGI programs and scripting languages. Servlets are extremely similar to proprietary server APIs (application programming interfaces), but because they are written in the Java programming language, they can be easily ported to any environment that supports the Java Servlet API. Since they run in the Java Virtual Machine (JVM), they bypass the security problems that affect the server APIs.

Servlets are run inside a servlet engine. Each individual servlet is run as a thread inside a Web server process. This is a much more efficient solution than multiple server processes implemented by CGI programs. By running in threads, servlets are also very scaleable, and as they are a part of the Web server process themselves, they can interact closely with the Web server.

Servlets are extremely powerful replacements for CGI programs. They can be used to extend to any type of server imaginable. The built-in thread and security support make servlets a robust tool for extending a server service.

All major Web servers now support servlets. The major drawback of using Java servlets is in their power. The Java programming language is at once both powerful and complicated, and learning Java is a formidable task for the average Web developer.

◆ 1.2 JavaServer Pages

JSP is an extremely powerful choice for Web development. JSP is a technology using server-side scripting that is actually translated into servlets, which are compiled before they are run. This gives developers a scripting interface to create powerful Java servlets.

JSP provides tags that allow developers to perform most dynamic content operations without writing complex Java code. Advanced developers can add the full power of the Java programming language to perform advanced operations in JSP.

1.2.1 Template Pages

Clearly, the most effective way to make a page respond dynamically would be to simply modify the static page. Ideally, special sections to the page could be added that would be changed dynamically by the server. In this case, pages become more like a page template for the server to process before sending. These are no longer normal Web pages; they are now server pages.

On a server page, the client requests a Web page, the server replaces some sections of a template with new data, and sends this newly modified page to the client (see Figure 1–1).

Since the processing occurs on the server, the client receives what appears to be static data. As far as the client is concerned there is no difference between a server page and a standard Web page. This creates a solution for dynamic pages that does not consume client resources and is completely browser-neutral.

1.2.2 Static Data vs. Dynamic Elements

Since JSP is designed around static pages, it can be composed of the same kind of static data as a standard Web page. JSP pages use HTML or XML to build the format and layout of a page. As long as a normal Web page can contain the data, so can a JSP page.

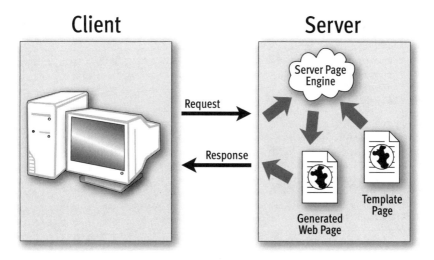

FIGURE 1–1 Server Page

To replace sections of a page, the server needs to be able to recognize the sections it needs to change. A JSP page usually has a special set of "tags" to identify a portion of the page that should be modified by the server. JSP uses the `<%` tag to note the start of a JSP section and the `%>` tag to note the end of a JSP section. JSP will interpret anything within these tags as a special section.

JSP pages usually contain a mixture of both static data and dynamic elements. It is important to understand the distinction between the two forms. Static data is never changed in the server page, and dynamic elements will always be interpreted and replaced before reaching the client.

1.2.3 A Simple JSP Page

Often, the easiest way to understand something is to see it. Script 1.1 shows a very simple JSP page.

Don't worry too much about what the JSP page is doing; that will be covered in later chapters. It is important to notice the two types of data in the page: static data and dynamic data. Understanding the difference between these builds an essential foundation for creating JSP pages.

Script 1.1
simpleDate.jsp

```
<!DOCTYPE HTML PUBLIC "-//W3C//DTD HTML 4.0 Final//EN">
<HTML>
<HEAD>
<TITLE>Stitch Magazine! - A simple date example</TITLE>
</HEAD>
<BODY COLOR=#ffffff>
<font face="Arial">
The current time is
<%= new java.util.Date() %>
</font>
</BODY></HTML>
```

When the client requests this JSP page, the client will receive a document as HTML. The translation is displayed in Figure 1–2.

When compiled and sent to the browser, the page should look like Figure 1–3.

1.2.4 JavaServer Pages

Most Web servers that understand JSP will look for a specific filename extension. Typically, any filename that ends in `.jsp` will be interpreted and processed by the JSP engine. Often, the actual

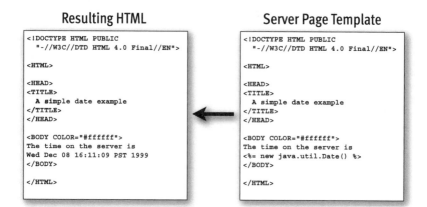

Resulting HTML

```
<!DOCTYPE HTML PUBLIC
  "-//W3C//DTD HTML 4.0 Final//EN">

<HTML>

<HEAD>
<TITLE>
 A simple date example
</TITLE>
</HEAD>

<BODY COLOR="#ffffff">
The time on the server is
Wed Dec 08 16:11:09 PST 1999
</BODY>

</HTML>
```

Server Page Template

```
<!DOCTYPE HTML PUBLIC
  "-//W3C//DTD HTML 4.0 Final//EN">

<HTML>

<HEAD>
<TITLE>
 A simple date example
</TITLE>
</HEAD>

<BODY COLOR="#ffffff">
The time on the server is
<%= new java.util.Date() %>
</BODY>

</HTML>
```

FIGURE 1–2 A Server Page into HTML Data

extension is configurable, but for the sake of clarity, this book will use .jsp throughout.

ESSENTIAL NOTE: JSP PAGES WITHOUT JSP TAGS
Since a JSP can handle the same static data as an HTML file, any HTML file can be changed to the extension .jsp. If the JSP server is running, these files will now run through the JSP engine. Without specific tags to identify dynamic sections, this document will come out exactly the same as the original HTML file, but it will take more resources because the JSP engine will attempt to parse and execute the file.

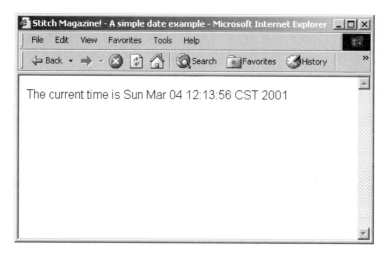

The current time is Sun Mar 04 12:13:56 CST 2001

FIGURE 1–3 A Simple JSP Page

◆ 1.3 The Power of Java

JSP inherits many of its advantages from the underlying Java programming language and Java servlet technology. It also has advantages over alternate methods of development by integrating into the component model. Beyond these advantages, the JSP specification is extremely well designed, enabling extensibility and integration with other languages and specifications.

1.3.1 Write Once, Run Anywhere

Because JSP utilizes the Java programming language, it automatically has many advantages. First and foremost is the high level of portability offered by Java's well-defined and accepted API. A JSP page developed on one platform can be deployed on a large number of systems. For example, a JSP page developed on a Windows NT system tested on the JSP Reference Implementation can be easily deployed on a Linux box running Allaire Software's JRun Application Server.

Further, JSP avoids the few troublesome areas of cross-platform Java development. Since JSP pages run on the server, applications do not need to be tested with several different client platforms, as is often necessary with Java applets. The sometimes troublesome GUI systems developed in Java, such as AWT and Swing, are also avoided in JSP.

1.3.2 The Java API

Probably one of the first things you'll notice when writing JSP is that you have the full power of the Java API. The core Java API offers the power of networking, multithreading, database connectivity, internationalization, image manipulation, object serialization, remote method invocation, CORBA access, and more. Standard extensions to Java, such as the Java Naming and Directory Interface (JNDI) and the Java Mail API, offer powerful extensions to Web applications.

With the Java classes, JavaBeans™, and Enterprise Java Beans™ (EJB) components offered by numerous software vendors, it is easy to add powerful code to Web applications. Using the JavaBeans component framework, JSP can form the presentation layer of multitier applications.

JSP can be written to communicate directly to applets, allowing the same code to be leveraged on both the server and client. This opens a whole new world of client/server application development.

1.3.3 Security and Safety

Another advantage inherited from the Java programming language is strong type safety. Unlike common scripting languages, JSP and the underlying Java Servlet API manipulate data in their native types instead of strings. Java also avoids many memory issues with automatic garbage collection and the absence of pointers.

Java is also known for its excellent exception handling. When an error occurs, JSP can safely catch the exception and notify the user, instead of potentially crashing the server. This built-in feature is considered far superior to the add-on extensions and modules often implemented in other Web application environments.

Finally, a Java application server can utilize the Java security manager, protecting itself from poorly written JSP that could potentially affect server performance or damage the host file system. The Java security manager controls rights to resources that could be used to damage the system, only allowing processes with the proper rights to gain access to protected resources. This is a fundamental part of the Java programming language.

1.3.4 Scalability

The Java programming language, as well as the Java Servlet API, adds several scalability components to JSP. After a JSP page is loaded, it generally is maintained in memory. When a new request comes in for the JSP page, the server makes a simple method invocation. This is very different from traditional CGI applications, which often spawn a process and an interpreter for every request. The underlying server handles multiple requests concurrently by utilizing separate threads, making JSP highly scalable.

When integrated into the JavaBean component framework, JSP becomes even more scalable. For example, a JDBC JavaBean can handle multiple requests from JSP and maintain a single, efficient connection to the back-end database. This is especially efficient when integrated with Enterprise JavaBeans, which add transaction and security services to Web applications, as well as middleware support for Java components.

1.3.5 Extensibility

Another area where JSP often outshines its competitors is in its extensibility. The JSP specification itself is an extension of the Java servlet extension. Within JSP, the specification can be extended to create custom tags. These tags allow the JSP "language" to be extended in a portable fashion. One good idea, for example, would be to create a custom tag library filled with embedded database queries. By making these tag libraries portable, and by giving them a common interface, JSP can express the component model internally.

The JSP specification authors also left room for further extensibility by making the elements utilized by JSP independent of any certain scripting language. Currently the JSP specification only supports the Java programming language for scripting, but JSP engines can choose to support other languages.

JSP's close relationship to the Extensible Markup Language (XML) is also very important, due to the extensibility and highly organized structure of XML. A properly formed JSP page can actually be written as a valid XML document. Simple XML generation can be done in JSP by using static templates. Dynamic XML generation can be done with custom tag components, JavaBeans, or Enterprise JavaBean components. XML can also be received as request data and sent directly to custom tag components, JavaBeans, or Enterprise JavaBean components.

1.3.6 Components

An extremely powerful feature of JSP is its ability to integrate into the JavaBean component framework. This opens the door for large-scale, enterprise applications created by development teams. As Web applications become more complex, utilizing the component nature of JSP helps break down the complex tasks into simpler, manageable modules. JSP helps separate presentation logic from business logic, and allows the separation of static and dynamic data.

Because of this component-centric nature, both Java programmers and non-Java programmers alike can utilize JSP. It allows Java programmers to make and use JavaBeans, and to create dynamic Web pages utilizing fine control over those beans. Non-Java programmers can use JSP tags to connect to Java-Beans created by experienced Java developers.

◆ 1.4 Recap

In closing, JSP offers significant benefits over legacy Web development technologies. Its use of the Java programming language gives it security, reliability, and access to a powerful API. Its memory and threading models offer significant speed enhancements. Additionally, JSP is built around a component model that helps separate business logic from presentation logic.

The next chapter, "Scripting Elements," takes an in-depth look at the JSP language itself.

2 Scripting Elements

chapter

IN THIS CHAPTER

- The Scriptlet Element
- Expression Element Syntax
- Declaration Element Syntax
- Embedded Control-Flow Statements
- Comment Syntax
- Scripting Elements Applied: `Calendar.jsp`
- Recap
- Advanced Project

Having seen the syntax of a simple JSP page, the next step is to get a better understanding of the different types of tags or scripting elements used in JSP. There are five basic types of elements, as well as a special format for comments.

The first three elements—scriptlets, expressions, and declarations—are collectively called scripting elements. The scriptlet element allows Java code to be embedded directly into a JSP page. An expression element is a Java language expression whose value is evaluated and returned as a string to the page. A declaration element is used to declare methods and variables that are initialized with the page.

ESSENTIAL NOTE: SCRIPTING LANGUAGE
The writers of the JSP specification did not define a requirement that
Java be the scripting language for a JSP page. Currently, the majority
of JSP engines only support the use of Java, but in the future, other
languages such as JavaScript, VBScript, or others could be used as the
scripting language.

The two other elements are actions and directives. Action elements provide information for the translation phase of the JSP
page, and consist of a set of standard, built-in methods. Custom
actions can also be created in the form of custom tags. This is a
feature of the JSP 1.1 and above specifications. Directive elements contain global information that is applicable to the
whole page.

It is also important to note that there are two different formats for most elements. The first type is called the JSP syntax. It
is based on the syntax of other server pages, so it might seem
very familiar. It is symbolized by: `<% script %>`. The JSP specification refers to this format as the "friendly" syntax, as it is meant
for hand-authoring. The second format is an XML standard format for creating JSP pages. This format is symbolized by:
`<jsp:element />`. While some find it more time-consuming to
author with the XML syntax, it would produce the same results.
While XML syntax is included here, JSP syntax is recommended
for authoring. Most of the examples in this book will be in the
JSP format.

◆ 2.1 The Scriptlet Element

JSP Syntax:
```
<% code %>
```

XML Syntax:
```
<jsp:Scriptlet > code </jsp:scriptlet>
```

The simplest type of JSP element is the scriptlet element. A scriptlet
element is simply a section of Java code encapsulated within the
opening and closing JSP tags. It is important to note that individual scriptlets cannot span multiple pages, and that all of the
scriptlets on a single page put together must form a valid block of
Java code. Scriptlets can produce output to the page, but don't

necessarily have to produce any output. If a scriptlet needs to produce output, it is generally done through the implicit out object.

ESSENTIAL NOTE: THE IMPLICIT OUT OBJECT

In the JSP 1.x specifications, out is an instance of the
javax.servlet.jsp.JspWriter class. The JspWriter object is created to buffer output. If a page needs to be buffered, all output goes
to the JspWriter object, and when the buffer is full or the page is
completed, a PrintWriter object is created to output the data. If
the page is not buffered, the JspWriter simply funnels the output
directly to a PrintWriter object. Both the print() and println()
methods perform the same function on JspWriter as they do with a
PrintWriter object. They take an object as an argument and send it
to the output stream. If necessary, the object is converted to a
String.

Script 2.1 shows a very simple implementation of a dynamic
JSP page utilizing a scriptlet. The JSP open tag (<%) begins the
Java fragment. The println() method of the implicit out object
is called. Within the println(), a new Date object is created. The
println() method returns a String comprised of the current
date in the format of the current locale and time zone.

Script 2.1
date.jsp

```
<!DOCTYPE HTML PUBLIC "-//W3C//DTD HTML 4.0 Final//EN">
<HTML>
<HEAD>
<TITLE>Stitch Magazine! - Current Date</TITLE>
</HEAD>
<BODY>

The current date is:
<% out.println(new java.util.Date()); %>

</BODY>
</HTML>
```

The output of this example should look similar to Figure 2–1.
It is important to note that the output of this Scriptlet shows the
date of the server, which may be very different from the date
where the client resides. A client-side technology such as
JavaScript would have to be used to print out the local date.

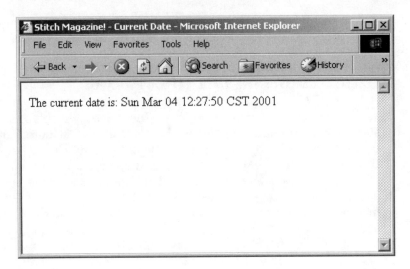

FIGURE 2–1 `date.jsp` Output

◆ 2.2 Expression Element Syntax

JSP Syntax:

```
<%= code %>
```

XML Syntax:

```
<jsp:expression > code </jsp:expression>
```

It turns out that printing the output of a Java fragment is one of the most common tasks utilized in JSP. Having several `out.println()` methods tends to be cumbersome. Realizing this, the authors of the JSP specification created the expression element.

An expression element begins with the standard JSP start tag, followed by an equals sign (`<%=`). Take a look at Script 2.2 to see the previous example of printing the current date, only this time as an expression element.

Script 2.2
date2.jsp

```
<!DOCTYPE HTML PUBLIC "-//W3C//DTD HTML 4.0 Final//EN">

<HTML>
<HEAD>
<TITLE>Stitch Magazine! - Current Date</TITLE>
</HEAD>
```

```
<BODY>

The current date is:
<%= new java.util.Date() %>

</BODY>
</HTML>
```

Notice that the Java fragment does not end in a semicolon, as do standard Java statements. The JSP engine takes the Java fragment and evaluates it. It then returns the output of the statement to the implicit `out` object. Notice that the `out.println()` method is removed, and immediately after the opening JSP tag, there is an equals sign. This code returns exactly the same result as our previous example (see Figure 2–1).

At first glance, the functionality of the expression element seems simple. It appears to just wrap an `out.print()` method around the Java fragment. This is in fact true. However, the rich set of data types in Java distinguishes it from other scripting languages such as JavaScript or VBScript. While other languages deal mostly with strings, Java can deal with numerous data types, as well as user-creatable data types. So, how can it print the value of an expression that does not return a `String`?

The `println()` (as well as `print()`) methods of the `Jsp-Writer` class are overloaded to accept most common data types as input. Overloading is the process of giving functions the same name. This is possible as long as the functions differ in number, type, or order of their parameters. The data type is then converted to a `String`, most often using the `String.valueOf()` method. The resulting `String` is translated into bytes and written in exactly the manner of the `write(int)` method of the `java.io.Writer` object.

◆ 2.3 Declaration Element Syntax

JSP Syntax:

`<%! code %>`

XML Syntax:

`<jsp:declaration>code</jsp:declaration>`

The third type of scripting element is the declaration element. The purpose of a declaration element is to initialize variables and methods and make them available to other declarations, scriptlets, and expressions. Variables and methods created within

declaration elements are effectively nonlocalized, or "global."
The syntax of the declaration element begins with the standard
JSP open tag followed by an exclamation point (<%!).

A declaration element must be a complete Java statement. It
ends with a semicolon, just as a scriptlet element does. It is also
important to note that declaration elements do not produce any
output, as expression and scriptlet elements do.

Script 2.3 rewrites our previous two examples utilizing a declaration element. The standard JSP open tag, followed by the exclamation point symbolize the beginning of the declaration
element. Here, the new method, called PrintDate(), is declared
as a public method, which returns a Date object. The body of the
method simply returns the Date object.

Since a declaration element cannot send output to the out
object, an expression element is called to return the output of the
PrintDate() method. Again, the resulting page sent to the client
is the same (see Figure 2–1).

Script 2.3
date3.jsp

```
<!DOCTYPE HTML PUBLIC "-//W3C//DTD HTML 4.0 Final//EN">

<%! public java.util.Date PrintDate()
    {
        return(new java.util.Date());
    }
%>

<HTML>
<HEAD>
<TITLE>Stitch Magazine! - Current Date</TITLE>
</HEAD>
<BODY>

The current date is:
<%= PrintDate() %>

</BODY>
</HTML>
```

◆ 2.4　Embedded Control-Flow Statements

These three scripting elements themselves are an extremely powerful set of tools to work with. One of their most powerful features
comes from one simple fact: together, scripting elements must

form a complete Java statement. The key word is "together." Blocks of Java code do not have to be kept within one Scriptlet or Expression. This adds the ability to use Java control-flow statements directly within HTML. While other tools, such as JavaScript, can add data to a Web page, they cannot directly control the static HTML content.

This means that decision-making, looping, and exception blocks can be added directly into HTML. The blocks do not have to be in a single scriptlet or expression, but can be broken up into several elements distributed throughout the HTML code. See Script 2.4.

Script 2.4
ControlFlow.jsp

```
<!DOCTYPE HTML PUBLIC "-//W3C//DTD HTML 4.0 Final//EN">
<%
        java.util.Calendar thisCal =
              java.util.Calendar.getInstance();
        int day   = thisCal.get(thisCal.DAY_OF_WEEK);

        String[] wordArray = {"The", "quick", "brown",
                              "fox", ". . ."};
        String[] colorArray = {"red", "green", "blue",
                               "orange", "black"};

        java.util.Random rand = new java.util.Random();
        int randomNumber = rand.nextInt(2);
%>
<HTML>
<HEAD>
<TITLE>Stitch Magazine! - Control Flow Statements</TITLE>
</HEAD>
<BODY>

<TABLE BORDER="1" WIDTH="420" CELLPADDING="3" CELLSPACING="0">
<TR><TD BGCOLOR="#AAAAAA" ALIGN="center">
<FONT FACE="Arial" SIZE="+3" COLOR="white">
Control Flow Statements</FONT>
</TD></TR>
<TR><TD>

<!-- ************************************************************ -->
<H3>Decision Making Statements</H3>
<B><code>if . . . else</code> Statements</B><BR>
<CENTER>
<%  if (day == 1 | day == 7) { %>
    <FONT FACE="Arial" COLOR="red" SIZE="+1">
    It's the weekend!</FONT>
<%  } else { %>
```

```
      <FONT FACE="Arial" COLOR="red" SIZE="+1">
      Still in the work week.
      </FONT>
<%  } %>
</CENTER>


<!-- ******************************************************** -->
<BR><B><code>switch . . . case</code> Statements</B><BR>

<CENTER>
<FONT FACE="Arial" COLOR="blue">The current day is:<br></FONT>
<% switch (day) {
   case 1: %>
     <FONT FACE="Arial" COLOR="blue" SIZE="+1">Sunday</FONT>
     <% break;
   case 2: %>
     <FONT FACE="Arial" COLOR="blue" SIZE="+1">Monday</FONT>
     <% break;
   case 3: %>
     <FONT FACE="Arial" COLOR="blue" SIZE="+1">Tuesday</FONT>
     <% break;
   case 4: %>
     <FONT FACE="Arial" COLOR="blue" SIZE="+1">Wednesday</FONT>
     <% break;
   case 5: %>
     <FONT FACE="Arial" COLOR="blue" SIZE="+1">Thursday</FONT>
     <% break;
   case 6: %>
     <FONT FACE="Arial" COLOR="blue" SIZE="+1">Friday</FONT>
     <% break;
   case 7: %>
     <FONT FACE="Arial" COLOR="blue" SIZE="+1">Saturday</FONT>
     <% break;
   default: %>
     <FONT FACE="Arial" COLOR="blue" SIZE="+1">Error! Bad day!
     </FONT>
     <% break;
   } %>
</CENTER>

</TD></TR><TR><TD>

<!-- ******************************************************** -->
<H3>Loop Statements</H3>
<B><code>for</code> Statements</B><BR>
<CENTER>
<% for (int fontSize=1; fontSize <= 5; fontSize++) { %>
   <FONT FACE="Arial" COLOR="green" SIZE="<%= fontSize %>">
     The Quick Brown Fox . . .</FONT><br>
<% } %>
```

```
</CENTER>

<!-- ********************************************************** -->
<BR><B><code>while</code> Statements</B><BR>
<CENTER>
<% int counter = 0; %>
<% while( counter <= 4) { %>
   <FONT FACE="Arial"
        COLOR="<%=colorArray[counter] %>" SIZE="+1">
   <%= wordArray[counter] %></FONT>
   <% counter++; %>
<% } %>
</CENTER>

</TD></TR><TR><TD>

<!-- ********************************************************** -->
<H3>Exception Statements</H3>
<B><code>try . . . catch</code> Statements</B><BR>
<CENTER>
<FONT FACE="Arial" COLOR="orange">Trying to divide by
this random number: <%= randomNumber %></FONT><BR>
<% try { %>
    <% int result = 100 / randomNumber; %>
    <FONT FACE="Arial" COLOR="orange" SIZE="+1">Success!</FONT>
<% } catch (Exception e) { %>
    <FONT FACE="Arial"
         COLOR="orange" SIZE="+1">Failure! </FONT>
    <FONT FACE="Arial" COLOR="red" SIZE="+1">
    Error Message: <%= e.getMessage() %></FONT>
<% } %>
</CENTER>
</TD></TR>
</TABLE>

</BODY>
</HTML>
```

When run, `ControlFlow.jsp` creates a Web page similar to Figure 2–2. `ControlFlow.jsp` starts out with the common HTML DOCTYPE statement. It then has a scriptlet that defines a few variables that will be used to demonstrate the abilities of control-flow statements.

```
java.util.Calendar thisCal =
     java.util.Calendar.getInstance();
int day   = thisCal.get(thisCal.DAY_OF_WEEK);

String[] wordArray = {"The", "quick", "brown",
                      "fox", ". . .,"};
```

```
String[] colorArray = {"red", "green", "blue",
            "orange",  "black"};
java.util.Random rand = new java.util.Random();
int randomNumber = rand.nextInt(2);
```

The first variable, `thisCal`, is used to get an integer value of the day of the week and place it into the integer `day`. The next part of the scriptlet creates two `String` arrays. The final section creates an instance of `java.util.Random` and sets the value of `randomNumber` to a random number between 0 and 1.

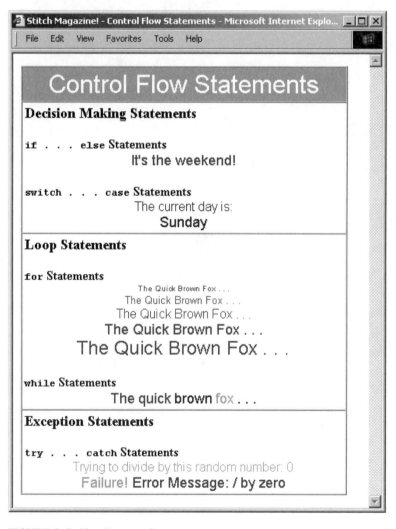

FIGURE 2–2 The Output of `ControlFlow.jsp`

The next section is some standard HTML to format the examples. After this section, three different table cells describe decision-making, looping, and exception statements.

2.4.1 Decision-Making Statements

There are two basic types of decision-making blocks in Java: if...else blocks and case blocks. Another type of block, called a branching statement, is very similar to a decision-making statement, but is used less frequently. The branching statements are symbolized by label: statements and the break and continue key words.

The if block starts out like an ordinary scriptlet, but the scriptlet is closed at each line with HTML text included between the scriptlet tags.

```
<%  if (day == 1 | day == 7) { %>
     <FONT FACE="Arial" COLOR="red" SIZE="+1">
     It's the weekend!</FONT>
<%  } else { %>
     <FONT FACE="Arial" COLOR="red" SIZE="+1">
     Still in the work week.
     </FONT>
<%  } %>
```

This means that the actual if block is spread over three different scriptlet tags. The three lines of static HTML text are actually the actions to take based on the condition. How does this work? Remembering back to the discussion about the expression element, the JSP engine simply wraps out.print() methods around the internal data in the Expression tag. The Java code is then evaluated and sent to the out object. The JSP engine handles template data, or raw HTML data, the same way. It simply wraps it in out.print() methods. This is how the resulting Java program will see this block of code:

```
if (day == 1 | day == 7) {
  <FONT FACE="Arial" COLOR="red" SIZE="+1">
  It's the weekend!</FONT>
} else {
  <FONT FACE="Arial" COLOR="red" SIZE="+1">
  Still in the work week.
  </FONT>
}
```

Could this section of Java code simply be enclosed in a scriptlet tag to produce the same result? Certainly. There are benefits gained from separating the template data from the application logic. Simply writing the block above in a scriptlet would mean that either the Java coder would need to know HTML and graphic design, or they would have to convert someone else's HTML to this format every time it changes. JSP can do this, saving time and effort and defining a division of labor.

Now take a look at the case block example:

```
<% switch (day) {
    case 1: %>
      <FONT FACE="Arial" COLOR="blue" SIZE="+1">Sunday</FONT>
      <% break;
    case 2: %>
      <FONT FACE="Arial" COLOR="blue" SIZE="+1">Monday</FONT>
      <% break;
    case 3: %>
      <FONT FACE="Arial" COLOR="blue" SIZE="+1">Tuesday</FONT>
      <% break;
    case 4: %>
      <FONT FACE="Arial" COLOR="blue" SIZE="+1">Wednesday</FONT>
      <% break;
    case 5: %>
      <FONT FACE="Arial" COLOR="blue" SIZE="+1">Thursday</FONT>
      <% break;
    case 6: %>
      <FONT FACE="Arial" COLOR="blue" SIZE="+1">Friday</FONT>
      <% break;
    case 7: %>
      <FONT FACE="Arial" COLOR="blue" SIZE="+1">Saturday</FONT>
      <% break;
    default: %>
      <FONT FACE="Arial" COLOR="blue" SIZE="+1">Error! Bad day!
      </FONT>
      <% break;
    } %>
```

While on the surface this code may seem more complex than the if statement, the logic is actually the same. Each line of the case statement is enclosed in a scriptlet tag. Eighteen actual scriptlet tags and eight HTML strings contribute to this single case block—all of this to produce one line of HTML code!

2.4.2 Loop Statements

There are three basic types of looping blocks in Java: for, while, and do...while blocks. First, take a look at the for example in Script 2.4:

```
<% for (int fontSize=1; fontSize <= 5; fontSize++) { %>
   <FONT FACE="Arial" COLOR="green" SIZE="<%= fontSize %>">
%>">
      The Quick Brown Fox . . .</FONT><br>
<% } %>
```

Once the concept is understood, the logic is quite clear. The JSP elements and static HTML data work in unison to form a single `for` block. One difference here is the use of an expression tag (`<%=  ...  %>`). This is mainly for convenience, but again, it shows the versatility of JSP. Each time through the loop, the size of the font is increased by one.

The `for` statement can be seen as a very valuable tool. For example, a table can be created with an unknown number of rows. The number of rows could be determined from a request variable, and each row printed in the `for` loop with the appropriate variables substituted.

Now take a look at the `while` loop:

```
<% int counter = 0; %>
<% while( counter <= 4) { %>
   <FONT FACE="Arial"
         COLOR="<%=colorArray[counter] %>" SIZE="+1">
   <%= wordArray[counter] %></FONT>
   <% counter++; %>
<% } %>
```

Once again, HTML template data and JSP elements are mixed to create a valid Java statement. An expression is mixed in directly with the HTML data. This example uses Java arrays corresponding to the number of times the HTML data is to be printed. This structure could be used to display a variable set of HTML constructs depending on a request variable.

2.4.3 Exception Statements

Exception statements, using the `try...catch...finally` key words, are powerful constructs in Java. There is even a built-in method in JSP to handle general exceptions caught by the JSP engine.

Any situation that involves getting data from a user and using it in programming logic must be very careful. Even with data validation, it is often necessary to catch any problem thrown from bad input. In this situation, the exception block excels. Take a look at the following exception example:

```
<% try { %>
   <% int result = 100 / randomNumber; %>
```

```
    <FONT FACE="Arial" COLOR="orange" SIZE="+1">Success!</FONT>
<% } catch (Exception e) { %>
    <FONT FACE="Arial"
        COLOR="orange" SIZE="+1">Failure! </FONT>
    <FONT FACE="Arial" COLOR="red" SIZE="+1">
    Error Message: <%= e.getMessage() %></FONT>
<% } %>
```

Again, the blending of HTML data and JSP tags works well. The number 100 is divided by a randomly generated number between zero and one. Approximately half of the times this page is loaded, zero will be chosen for the random number, which creates a divide by zero error. The simple way to handle this exception is to enclose it in a `try` block. This way, if the exception occurs, the page is still rendered and the error message can be displayed.

`ControlFlow.jsp` is a good example of how JSP scripting elements add power to static HTML data. HTML pages can be displayed with decision-making, looping, and exception-handling statements. At the same time, they separate the presentation logic from the business logic, allowing for design and programming teams to work separately to produce tightly integrated applications.

◆ 2.5 Comment Syntax

JSP Syntax:

```
<%-- comment --%>
```

XML Syntax:

```
<!-- comment -->
```

There are two different types of comments in JSP. The difference between the types of comments lies in whether the comments are viewable after the JSP engine parses the JSP. The first type of comment is the standard HTML (and XML) comment, which is delineated by: `<!-- comment -->`. This comment is ignored by both the JSP engine and the browser, and is left intact. In effect, all comments in HTML style are considered template data. To see a comment like this, simply choose to view source in an HTML browser.

The second type of comment is called a JSP or "hidden" comment. The JSP engine removes JSP comments before a page is built. Thus, it is viewable on the JSP page on the server, but not on the browser. The JSP comment syntax is `<%-- comment --%>`. JSP comments are treated as element data, and are parsed by the server.

There are a couple of interesting things that can be done with comments that are extremely useful when developing JSP pages. First, JSP elements can be included within HTML comments. This might be helpful in debugging a script. An expression statement can be included in a comment to show the current value of a variable. This would not be viewable on the HTML page, but it would be viewable via the browser's "View Source" function.

ESSENTIAL NOTE: JSP COMMENTS

Some implementations of JSP engines do not handle JSP comments correctly. They simply remove the <% and %> tags and leave the comment as-is. This can cause a compile-time error. A simple work-around is to create the comments as scriptlet elements. For example:

```
<% // This is a comment in a Scriptlet  %>
```

This creates a Java statement that is commented out. It behaves like a JSP comment, and is not sent to the browser. This format should work on any platform.

The second helpful task is commenting out JSP code so it doesn't get compiled. Surrounding normal JSP elements with a JSP comment causes the JSP engine to ignore the JSP code. This allows the selective removal of certain parts of the JSP page.

Take a look at Script 2.5 and Figure 2–3 to see how different comments will be displayed. Script 2.5 is the source on the server, and Figure 2–3 is the source viewed on the client. In a normal browser window, nothing would be displayed. Anything displayed on the server side that is surrounded by the JSP comment syntax is removed completely. Also notice that the JSP element that was included inside the JSP comment was not executed.

Script 2.5
`comments.jsp` on the Server

```
<!DOCTYPE HTML PUBLIC "-//W3C//DTD HTML 4.0 Final//EN">

<HTML>
<HEAD>
<TITLE>Stitch magazine! - Using Comments</TITLE>
```

```
</HEAD>
<BODY>

<!-- This is a HTML Style comment -->

<%-- This is a JSP Style comment --%>

<!-- In this HTML comment. I can dynamically retrieve the
URL of the current page:  <%= request.getRequestURI()%> -->

<%--
Here I am commenting out the following JSP code:
<%= request.getServerName()%>
--%>

</BODY>
</HTML>
```

All items that were inside HTML-style comments were treated as template data and left alone, with the exception of the JSP element inside the HTML comment, which was parsed and executed.

If the `request.getRequestURI()` and `request.getServer-Name()` bits of code seem confusing, don't worry. These expressions are calling methods of the built-in JSP request object. `request.getRequestURI()` returns the relative URL of the current page, and `request.getServerName()` returns the name of the server receiving the Web page.

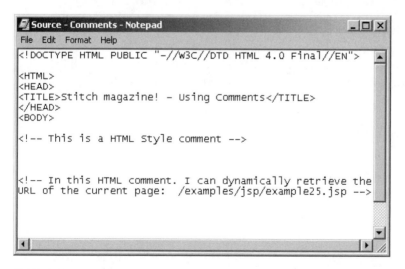

FIGURE 2–3 `comments.jsp` on the Client (View Source)

ESSENTIAL NOTE: `request` OBJECT

The `request` object, just like the `out` object, is an implicit object to the JSP page. It represents the request parameters associated with the page. This can include query strings (`GET` requests) and encoded post requests (`POST` requests), as well as several other pieces of information sent with the HTTP request.

◆ 2.6 Scripting Elements Applied:

`Calendar.jsp`

After seeing scriptlets, declarations, and expressions, it is obvious that very complex applications can be created with just these three elements. While these three elements are very similar to elements in other server pages technology, JSP has the added benefit of a full-featured programming language, Java.

ESSENTIAL NOTE: THE JAVA CALENDAR OBJECT

The `java.util.Calendar` object is new to the Java 1.1 and above API specifications. Previous to the 1.1 spec, the features of the `Calendar` object (as well as the features of the `DateFormat` object) were included in the Java `Date` object. The `Date` object represents a single moment in time with millisecond precision. It represents a major leap forward beyond older programming languages, where dates are represented as text strings. The absence of Year 2000 bugs with Java is a testament to this fact.

Unfortunately, the `Date` object was not very easy to internationalize. Specifically, converting between `Date` objects and integer fields such as YEAR, DAY, and HOUR is not very straightforward, especially when needing to format a single `Date` object to different locales and calendar systems. Thus, the `Calendar` object was created. It is an abstract class that can be subclassed with specific calendar systems. The example will use the `GregorianCalendar` subclass, which is built-in to the 1.1 and above API specs. It also uses the `DateFormat` class to format a representation of the current date to title our HTML calendar.

Script 2.6 is a good example of a real-world JSP use of expressions, declarations, and scriptlets, as well as utilizing a powerful feature of Java not seen in JavaScript, VBScript, and other scripting languages. Script 2.6 creates an HTML calendar, created from the Java `Calendar` object.

Script 2.6
`Calendar.jsp` on the Server

```
<!DOCTYPE HTML PUBLIC "-//W3C//DTD HTML 4.0 Final//EN">

<%!
  public String FormatTitle(java.util.Calendar thisCal) {
    java.text.SimpleDateFormat formatter =
   new java.text.SimpleDateFormat ("MMMMMMMMM d, yyyy");

    return (formatter.format(thisCal.getTime()));
  }
%>

<%
  java.util.Calendar currentCal =
       java.util.Calendar.getInstance();
%>

<HTML>
<HEAD>
<TITLE>Stitch Magazine! - Calendar</TITLE>
<STYLE TYPE="text/css">
<!--
TD {
  font-family: Arial, Helvetica, sans-serif;
  font-size: 10pt; text-align: center;
}

.currentDay {
  color: #FF0000; background-color: #EEEEEE;
}

.otherDay {
  color: #666699; background-color: #EEEEEE;
}

.dayHeading {
  font-size: 9pt; color: #666699;
}

.titleStyle {
  font-size: 14pt; color: #FFFFFF;
  background-color: #666699; text-align: center;
  font-weight: bold;
}

-->
</STYLE>
</HEAD>
```

```
<BODY>

<TABLE BORDER='0' CELLPADDING='1' CELLSPACING='2'>
  <TR><TD CLASS='titleStyle' COLSPAN='7'>
      <%= FormatTitle(currentCal) %>
  </TD></TR>

  <TR>
    <TD WIDTH=14% CLASS='dayHeading'>SUN</TD>
    <TD WIDTH=14% CLASS='dayHeading'>MON</TD>
    <TD WIDTH=14% CLASS='dayHeading'>TUE</TD>
    <TD WIDTH=14% CLASS='dayHeading'>WED</TD>
    <TD WIDTH=14% CLASS='dayHeading'>THU</TD>
    <TD WIDTH=14% CLASS='dayHeading'>FRI</TD>
    <TD WIDTH=14% CLASS='dayHeading'>SAT</TD>
  </TR>


<%  // Set the current day of the month
    int currentDay = currentCal.get(currentCal.DAY_OF_MONTH);

    // Calculate the total days in the month
    int daysInMonth =
        currentCal.getActualMaximum(currentCal.DAY_OF_MONTH);


// Calculate the day of the week for the first
    currentCal.set(currentCal.DAY_OF_MONTH, 1);
    int dayOfWeek = currentCal.get(currentCal.DAY_OF_WEEK);

    // Prefill the calendar with blank spaces
    if (dayOfWeek != 1) {
      out.println("    <TD COLSPAN=" +
        (dayOfWeek-1) + "> </TD>");
    }

    // Fill in dates
    for (int day=1; day <= daysInMonth; day++) {

      if (day == currentDay) {
        out.println("    <TD CLASS='currentDay'>"
        + day + "</TD>");
      } else {
        out.println("    <TD CLASS='otherDay'>"
        + day + "</TD>");
      }

      if (dayOfWeek == 7) {
        out.println("  </TR>\n\n  <TR>");
        dayOfWeek = 1;
```

```
      } else {
        dayOfWeek++;
      }
    }

    // Postfill the calendar with blank spaces
    if ((7-dayOfWeek) != 0) {
      out.println("    <TD COLSPAN=" + (8-dayOfWeek)
        + "> </TD>");
    }
%>
</TR>
</TABLE>

</BODY>
</HTML>
```

When run, `Calendar.jsp` creates a Web page similar to Figure 2–4.

`Calendar.jsp` starts out with the standard HTML document identification string, and then defines a method called `FormatTitle()` in a declaration element. One of the first things to notice here is the explicit naming of the `java.util.Calendar` and `java.text.SimpleDateFormat` objects. Without `import` statements, there is no way to use the shorter alias for these objects. `import` statements cannot simply be included in a scriptlet, as the Java specification states they must appear at the very beginning of the Java code. JSP pages, being transformed into Java

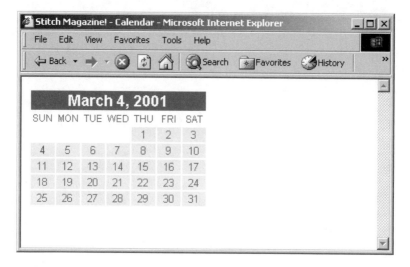

FIGURE 2–4 `Calendar.jsp` on the Server

servlet programs, cannot guarantee where a scriptlet will actually be placed in the Java program. import statements can be used within the page directive, which is covered in Chapter 3, "ActionElements." Using the full domain name, while less common, is a perfectly legal way of specifying objects.

The FormatTitle() method receives a Calendar object and returns a String with the current date formatted as specified. A Date or Calendar object must be converted to a string to be displayed in HTML. Earlier, the Date object was displayed by utilizing the println() or print() methods of the JspWriter object. The println() and print() methods are very smart. Realizing they are being sent a Date object, they automatically convert the Date object to a String using the String.valueOf(Date) method. This does the job of converting the Date object to a String, but only with the default format.

```
<%!
  public String FormatTitle(java.util.Calendar thisCal) {
    java.text.SimpleDateFormat formatter =
    new java.text.SimpleDateFormat ("MMMMMMMMM d, yyyy");

    return (formatter.format(thisCal.getTime())));
  }
%>
```

For the title of the HTML calendar, a shortened version is desired, only displaying the month, day, and year. To do this, the SimpleDateFormat class is used. Similar to the Calendar class, SimpleDateFormat's features were originally part of the Date object before Java 1.1. SimpleDateFormat takes a text string that specifies the String format desired for the date. First, the SimpleDateFormat object is created and is labeled formatter. Then, the format() method of the SimpleDateFormat object is called and applied to the Calendar object received. This object is called thisCal. As the format() method returns a string, it is simply inserted into the return method of the FormatTitle() method to return the current date in the specified format.

The format of this text string is based on the ISO 8601 date and time standard. It is also very similar to the string used by the ANSI C function strftime() and the UNIX date command. The format string here is: "MMMMMMMMM d, yyyy". The M stands for the month, both numeric and alphabetic representations. If there are more than three Ms, the method decides the alphabetic version is desired and fills in as many characters as there are Ms, ignoring any extra Ms for short month names. There are nine Ms listed to make sure every letter of the month is used, as the longest month (September) has nine characters.

Next there is a d, representing the numeric version of the day of the month, whether one or two digits. Finally, there are four ys. This represents the year. If three or less ys are specified, the date is returned in a two-digit format (not Year 2000-compliant). Four are specified here to specify the four-digit version.

It is important to note that while this method was listed at the top of the JSP page for convenience, it could have been placed anywhere on the page and supplied the same desired results. While it will be included as a part of the JSP page's class file, it is a separate and standalone method.

Next comes the creation of the Calendar object within a scriptlet:

```
<%
  java.util.Calendar currentCal =
        java.util.Calendar.getInstance();
%>
```

Again note the explicit naming of the Calendar object, as there is no import statement specified. Also note that here the order is very important. The Calendar object cannot be referenced anywhere in the page until it is initialized. The getInstance() method of the Calendar object creates a new Calendar object, assigning it the current date and time. The new Calendar object is named currentCal.

Now comes the standard HTML, HEAD, and TITLE tags. These tags are followed by some style definitions. These definitions are part of cascading style sheets (CSS), which are part of the HTML 4.0 specification.

```
<STYLE TYPE="text/css">
<!--
TD {
  font-family: Arial, Helvetica, sans-serif;
  font-size: 10pt; text-align: center;
}

.currentDay {
  color: #FF0000; background-color: #EEEEEE;
}

.otherDay {
  color: #666699; background-color: #EEEEEE;
}
```

```
.dayHeading {
   font-size: 9pt; color: #666699;
}

.titleStyle {
   font-size: 14pt; color: #FFFFFF;
   background-color: #666699; text-align: center;
   font-weight: bold;
}

-->
</STYLE>
```

There are five different styles listed. The first one, TD, will match the specified style to any TD tag occurring in the HTML page. The HTML table construct is used to create the calendar. currentDay specifies the style used by the table element that contains the current day. The current day is differentiated here with a red font. otherDay specifies any other day in the table. dayHeading designates a style for the column labels of the days of the week, and titleStyle designates the style used for the calendar title.

After the style definitions is the beginning of the table construct that will create the HTML calendar. Included in the first table row definition, which spans all seven rows, is the following JSP expression:

```
<%= FormatTitle(currentCal) %>
```

This calls the method defined earlier in the page. It sends the currentCal Calendar object and returns a String formatted to be the calendar title.

The next row simply prints the static three-letter representations of each day of the week. After this row comes the meat of this JSP page, the scriptlet that actually creates the HTML calendar. To create a calendar, two pieces of information are needed: the number of days in the current month and what day of the week the first day falls on. Additionally, the current day must be recorded if it is to be highlighted with a red font. To obtain these values, the get() and set() methods of the Calendar object are called. The Calendar object has several fields that define information that can be retrieved via the get() method.

The first line of the scriptlet creates a new integer called currentDay:

```
<%  // Set the current day of the month
   int currentDay = currentCal.get(currentCal.DAY_OF_MONTH);
```

Here, the `Calendar` object named `currentCal` calls its `get()` method and sends the field `DAY_OF_MONTH`. This field stands for the current day of the month, and the `get()` method returns this value, which is assigned to `currentDay`.

Next comes the number of days in the month. The new integer is aptly named `daysInMonth`. Similar to the `get()` method called to retrieve the current day, the field name `DAY_OF_MONTH` is called, only this time it is sent in a special method of the `Calendar` object called `getActualMaximum()`.

```
// Calculate the totals days in the month
int daysInMonth =
currentCal.getActualMaximum(currentCal.DAY_OF_MONTH);
```

This method returns the maximum value for the given field, and since the maximum days in the month is requested, it returns the total number of days in the month.

The third piece of information needed is the day of the week for the first day of the month. The simplest way to do this is to change the current day of the month in the `Calendar` object created to the first day of the month. This is done through the `Calendar set()` method. The two values sent of the `set()` method are the field value to be changed and the new value. Then, the `get()` method of the `Calendar` class can be called with the field specific to the day of the week.

```
// Calculate the day of the week for the first
currentCal.set(currentCal.DAY_OF_MONTH, 1);
int dayOfWeek =
   currentCal.get(currentCal.DAY_OF_WEEK);
```

It is important to note that the day of the week starts with 1 instead of 0, as do many `date` methods in Java. Most likely, this is to match the lack of a zero in the Gregorian calendar.

Now that the needed information is obtained, the calendar can be generated. The first step is to generate blank spaces for the days preceding the first day of the month. The `COLSPAN` HTML tag makes this easy. A table definition is created and assigned the value of `dayOfWeek` minus 1. To be safe, this is wrapped in an `if` statement that makes sure a `COLSPAN` of zero is not specified.

```
// Prefill the calendar with blank spaces
if (dayOfWeek != 1) {
  out.println("    <TD COLSPAN=" +
      (dayOfWeek-1) + "> </TD>");
}
```

Now the table elements that contain dates can be printed. This is done by using a `for` statement that starts at 1 and ends when the value of `daysInMonth` is reached.

```
// Fill in dates
    for (int day=1; day <= daysInMonth; day++) {

        if (day == currentDay) {
            out.println("    <TD CLASS='currentDay'>"
            + day + "</TD>");
        } else {
            out.println("    <TD CLASS='otherDay'>"
            + day + "</TD>");
        }

        if (dayOfWeek == 7) {
            out.println("  </TR>\n\n  <TR>");
    dayOfWeek = 1;
        } else {
            dayOfWeek++;
        }
    }
```

Two `if` statements are in the `for` loop. The first prints the current day. If it is equal to the `currentDay`, it specifies the CSS style that contains the red font. Otherwise, it specifies the `otherDay` style. The second `if` statement checks to see if the current `dayOfWeek` integer is equal to seven, and if it is, it closes the current table row and creates a new one. It also resets the `dayOfWeek` integer to one. If `dayOfWeek` is not equal to seven, it increments `dayOfWeek` by one.

To finish up this scriptlet, the closing empty table elements need to be filled in. This is accomplished by specifying another table element with a `COLSPAN` attribute to fill the remaining cells. Again, an `if` statement is used to make sure that a value of zero is not used.

```
    // Postfill the calendar with blank spaces
    if ((7-dayOfWeek) != 0) {
        out.println("    <TD COLSPAN=" + (8-dayOfWeek)
            + "> </TD>");
    }
```

With closing `TABLE`, `BODY`, and `HTML` tags, the JSP page is complete.

One issue not covered in Script 2.6 is localization. As with the previous `Date` examples, our HTML calendar will show the calendar for the time and date of the server. This might be very different from the time and date of the browser viewing the JSP page.

One way to solve this issue is to make the calendar object configurable by the viewer, such as creating a form where the local date could be set. This information could then be stored in a cookie or user database. This is a common issue with personalization and portal sites.

Another issue not covered is specific ways of viewing the Gregorian calendar. For example, in France, the first day of the week is traditionally Monday, whereas in Script 2.6 follows the American tradition of listing Sunday as the first day of the week.

`Calendar.jsp` is a good example of using scripting elements. It uses a method that is enclosed in a declaration. It utilizes an expression to call the method and insert information into the `out` object. The bulk of the processing itself is done in scriptlets. The page is integrated into a HTML table that utilizes CSS. It uses a Java `Date` object, showing the power added to JSP by the Java programming language.

◆ 2.7 Recap

`Calendar.jsp` also gives clues to the other powerful features in JSP. For example, how can Java domains be imported? While `Calendar.jsp` creates a nice HTML calendar, the code itself is not very reusable or modular. What if several calendars are needed; should the code be copied several times? The next chapters answer these questions by revealing further features of JSP. They reveal JSP resource actions, where the output of `Calendar.jsp` can be included in other JSP pages; they introduce the JSP bean actions, where code from JavaBeans can be used and reused in a component model; and, they describe the `page` and `include` directives, where changes to the underlying Java program that is created from the JSP page can be specified.

◆ 2.8 Advanced Project

As an advanced project, allow the user to select whether or not they prefer to see the calendar in "French" or "English" format, where the day optionally starts with Monday for the "French" format and Sunday for the "English" format. This will introduce new issues with keeping server-side information, which is covered in later chapters.

3 Action Elements

Action elements are very different from scripting elements. There is only one syntax for action element, as they conform to the XML standard:

Syntax:
```
<jsp:action_name />
```

Action elements are basically predefined functions. The JSP specification comes with several built-in actions, and with JSP specification 1.1, custom tags can be created through the jsp:taglib directive. An action element can modify the output stream, as well as create and use objects. Another interesting feature of the Action element is that the request object of the JSP page can directly influence its actions.

Following the XML standard, action elements can also have attributes, which is also different from the other standard elements. Attributes are a part of the action element tag and follow the jsp:action_name text. For example:

```
<jsp:action_name attribute="value" />.
```

◆ 3.1 `id` and `scope` **Attributes**

There are two attributes that are common to all action elements: the `id` attribute and the `scope` attribute. The `id` attribute uniquely identifies the action element, and allows the action to be referenced inside the JSP page. If the action creates an instance of an object, the `id` value can be used to reference it through the implicit object `PageContext`.

The second common attribute is the `scope` attribute, which identifies the life cycle of the action element. The `id` and `scope` attributes are directly related, as the `scope` attribute determines the lifespan of the object associated with the `id`. The `scope` attribute has four possible values: `page`, `request`, `session`, and `application`. Each of these values refers to an implicit object in the JSP page, similar to the `out` object referenced above.

When the `scope` attribute is set to `page`, it ties the object instantiated by the action tag to the `page` implicit object. The `page` object can be thought of as a synonym for "`this`" in the body of the page. An action with a scope of `page` can be thought of as a "one-time" object to be used and destroyed separately by each request to a JSP page.

With a `scope` attribute of `request`, the named object is made available from the `ServletRequest` object. This is accessed via the `getAttribute()` method.

With a value of `session`, the `scope` attribute stays alive while the session remains valid. The named object is also available from the `ServletRequest` object and is retrieved using the `getValue()` method.

A `scope` value of `application` associates the named object with the `ServletContext` object. This means that the object remains alive for the life of the current application or servlet. The application is normally kept alive unless the `destroy()` method is called, the JSP page or associated class files change, or the JSP engine is restarted.

Table 3–1 describes the four different scopes in greater detail.

TABLE 3–1 JSP Scope

Scope	Summary
page	Objects with *page* scope are accessible only as a part of the page in which they are created. References to objects with a scope of *page* are released after the response is sent back to the client from the JSP page or the request is forwarded somewhere else. References to objects with *page* scope are stored in the `pageContext` object.

Scope	Summary
request	Objects with *request* scope are accessible from pages processing the same request where they were created. When the request is processed, any object with a scope of *request* will be released. This is similar to the *page* scope, except that the object will still be accessible if the request object is passed to another JSP page. References to objects with *request* scope are stored in the request object.
session	Objects with *session* scope are accessible from pages processing requests that are in the same session as the one in which they were created. Before an object can be created with a scope of *session*, the JSP page must be declared session-aware (in the *page* directive). All references to an object with a scope of *session* are released after the associated session ends. References to objects with *session* scope are stored in the session object.
application	Objects with *application* scope are accessible from pages processing requests that are in the same application as the one in which they were created. All objects of *application* scope will be released when the JSP page is ended by the ServletContext, usually through the server shutdown, the page timeout, or a call to the jspDestroy() method. References to objects with *application* scope are stored in the application object.

◆ 3.2 Standard Actions

The JSP 1.0 and above specifications define six standard actions, which can be grouped into two distinct categories. Each of these actions should be available regardless of the JSP engine or Web server environment.

The first set of standard actions all tie together to utilize Java-Beans. useBean, setProperty, and getProperty are called the JavaBean actions. The second set of standard actions is called the resource actions. They allow the use of outside resources to be used within JSP.

3.2.1 The JavaBean Actions

The JavaBean actions differ from the resource actions because they all relate to using server-side JavaBeans within a JSP page. The useBean action is used to instantiate a new JavaBean for use later on the JSP page. The getProperty and setProperty actions are used to get and set properties that have been defined within a JavaBean.

The JavaBean actions fulfill a crucial role in the component model of JSP pages. By placing all business logic within Java-Beans and placing all presentation logic into the JSP page, Web applications can be written as separate, reusable, and scalable components. The JavaBean actions are the key to tying together the JavaBean business logic and JSP page presentation logic.

While the semantics of using JavaBean actions will be covered here, a detailed explanation of JavaBeans and Enterprise JavaBeans is covered in further chapters.

`<jsp:useBean>`

The `useBean` action finds or creates an instance of an object. It also associates this object with an implicit object specified by the scope attribute (`page`, `request`, `session`, and `application`). It identifies this new object with the value of the `id` attribute. It also creates a new scripting variable under the name of the `id` attribute that references the object.

The `useBean` action is quite versatile. It first searches for an existing object utilizing the `id` and `scope` variables. If an object is not found, it then tries to create the specified object. It can even be used to simply give a local name to an object defined somewhere else. This can be done by specifying the `type` attribute, but not using `class` or `beanName`.

Either the `class` attribute or the `type` attribute must be specified. The `class` attribute specifies the code from which the new object is to be created. The `type` attribute specifies the type of object, so that an existing object might be found. It is not legal to specify both `class` and `beanName` attributes. The `beanName` attribute identifies the new object with a Java bean. If both `class` and `type` are specified, `class` must be assignable to the specified type (see Table 3–2).

TABLE 3–2 `<jsp:useBean>` Attributes

id	The `id` attribute identifies the object within the specified scope's implicit object. It also creates a new scripting variable that is used to reference the object. Like any other scripting variable, it is case-sensitive and must conform to Java naming conventions. The `id` attribute is required.
scope	The `scope` attribute defines the implicit object within which the object's reference will be available. Legal values are `page`, `session`, `request`, and `application`. The default value is `page`.

`class`	`class` defines the implementation of the object. Without specifying the `class` name or `beanName`, the object must be available within the given scope.
`type`	The `type` attribute defines the type of scripting variable that is created. This allows the type of the scripting variable to be different, although related, to the type of the object it references. `type` is required to be the class itself, a superclass, or an interface of the class specified. If unspecified, the default is the type of the `class` attribute.
beanName	The name of the bean, as specified by the `instantiate()` method of the `java.beans.Beans` class. This can be specified at request time by an expression.

The `useBean` tag may or may not have a body. The following example illustrates a `useBean` action without a body:

```
<jsp:useBean id="newBean"
class="com.javadesktop.TableBean" />
```

Note the slash before the closing bracket, symbolizing the end of the tag. Now take a look at a similar `useBean` action that sets a property of the bean:

```
<jsp:useBean id="newBean"
class="com.javadesktop.TableBean">
    <jsp:setProperty name="newBean" property="border"
      value="0">
</jsp:useBean>
```

The proper way of defining a JavaBean with a combination of the `class`, `type`, and `beanName` attributes can be confusing. Table 3–3 describes the different combinations and whether or not they are valid.

TABLE 3–3 The `useBean` Tag

`class`	VALID. Class is valid by itself or with `type`.
`type`	VALID. Does not create a new object, but finds an object in the given `scope` and gives it a local name.
`beanName, type`	VALID. `type` is required if `beanName` is given.
`type, class`	VALID. `class` must be assignable to `type`.
`beanName`	INVALID.
`class, beanName`	INVALID.

`<jsp:setProperty>`

The `setProperty` action sets the properties of a bean. The bean must have been previously defined before this action. Table 3–4 shows the attributes of the `setProperty` action.

There are two basic ways to use the `setProperty` action: to set the value of a property to a request parameter, or to set the value with a string. When setting the value of a property to a string, either a string constant (a string literal enclosed by double quotes) or the value of another JSP expression can be used. For example:

```
<jsp:setProperty id="TableBean" property="border"
value="i+1" />

<jsp:setProperty id="TableBean" property="label"
   value=<%= TableName + "Label" %> />
```

The `param` attribute is used to set a property to the value of a request parameter. The value of the request parameter matching the `param` attribute value becomes the value of the property specified.

```
<jsp:setProperty id="TableBean" property="border"
   param="borderWidth" />
```

If the request parameter name and property name match, the `param` attribute can be omitted:

```
<jsp:setProperty id="TableBean" param="border" />
```

One of the most powerful features of the `setProperty` action is the ability to set the property attribute to asterisk (*).

```
<jsp:setProperty id="beanName" property="*" />
```

This causes the JSP engine to cycle through the request parameters sent to the JSP page. These parameters are part of the `ServletRequest` object. Using introspection, the JSP engine tries to match each parameter to a settable property of the bean. It finds a match when the request name matches the name of a bean property, and the type of the request value matches the type of the property value.

TABLE 3–4 `<jsp:setProperty>` Attributes

name	The name of the bean that has a property to be set. The bean must have been previously defined. With the JSP 1.0 specification and above, the bean must have been defined by using the `useBean` action. The property to be set must exist in the bean.
property	The `property` attribute is the name of the bean property to be set. If the `property` attribute is specified, but the `param` and `value` attributes are omitted, the property name is matched to a request parameter of the corresponding name.
param	The `param` attribute is the name of the request parameter whose value the property is to receive. If the parameter's value is null or the parameter does not exist, the `setProperty` action is ignored. A `param` attribute and a `value` attribute are not legal in the same `setProperty` action.
value	The value that is to be assigned to the given property. A `value` attribute and a `param` attribute are not legal in the same `setProperty` action.

`<jsp:getProperty>`

The `getProperty` action is used to retrieve the value of a given property and print it. This simply means inserting it into the implicit `out` object. The bean specified by the required `name` attribute must have been defined previously. In the JSP 1.0 specification and above, this means that the bean must have been defined with the `useBean` action.

The bean's property value is converted to a string using the `toString()` method of the specified object. The `getProperty` action has only two attributes, listed in Table 3–5. Both attributes are required. For example:

```
<jsp:getProperty name="TableBean" property="borderWidth" />
```

TABLE 3–5 `<jsp:getProperty>` Attributes

name	The name of the bean that has a property to be retrieved. The bean must have been previously defined. The property to be set must exist in the bean. This is a required attribute.
property	The `property` attribute is the name of the bean property to get. This is a required attribute.

3.2.2 The Resource Actions

Resource actions specify external resources that should be used with JSP. The `include` and `forward` actions allow interactions with other resources such as JSP pages, HTML pages, and XML pages. The `plugin` action allows automatically generated HTML to be written for specific browser constructs. This means that the appropriate construct (`<EMBED>` or `<OBJECT>`) will be created, the appropriate plugin will be downloaded (if needed), and the applet or JavaBean code will be executed.

There are two elements specifically associated with resource actions. `param` is an element used with the `plugin` action to specify the parameters to the JavaBean or applet. With the `include` and `forward` actions, the `param` element allows GET operands to be specified for the associated resource. (The `param` element is available for the `include` and `forward` actions beginning with the JSP 1.1 specification.) The `fallback` element is used with the `plugin` action if there is no appropriate construct for the particular browser, or if the applet or JavaBean fails to load for some other reason.

`<jsp:include>`

The `include` action can be used to insert the output of both static and dynamic pages into the current page. When the `include` action is encountered, the current processing is halted. The `JspWriter` `out` object is then released to receive the output of the resource identified with the `page` attribute. The output of the resource is completely received and any existing buffers flushed before the data is inserted into the `out` object. The output of the resource is not parsed by the JSP engine, but included "as-is".

This is very different from the `include` directive: `<%@ include file="filename" %>`. The `include` directive retrieves the resource specified by the `file` attribute and inserts it into the current JSP page before the page is parsed. The `include` directive is covered extensively later in this chapter.

TABLE 3–6 `<jsp:include>` Attributes

page	The relative URL of the page to be included. It must be an existing resource on the local Web server.
flush	The `flush` attribute determines whether the included resource has its buffer flushed before it is included. This attribute is required to have a Boolean value. With the JSP 1.0 and 1.1

specifications, "true" is the only legal attribute; "false" is allowable in the 1.2 specification. This is due to the structure of the underlying Java Servlet specification. This is a required attribute.

To use the `include` directive, simply specify a resource. This is done by setting the value of the `page` attribute (see Table 3–6 for the `include` directive attributes). The value must be on the local Web server and the `flush` attribute must be specified.

```
<jsp:include page="/data/footer.html" flush="true" />
```

With the JSP 1.1 specification, an optional `param` attribute can specify request parameters to be sent to the resource.

```
<jsp:include page="/data/login.jsp" flush="yes">
    <jsp:param name="user" value="Joe Blow" />
</jsp:include>
```

Script 3.1 demonstrates including the previous date example in a new JSP page:

Script 3.1
`include.jsp`

```
<!DOCTYPE HTML PUBLIC "-//W3C//DTD HTML 4.0 Final//EN">

<HTML>
<HEAD>
<TITLE>Stitch Magazine! - Using Includes</TITLE>
</HEAD>
<BODY>

<P>Here I am including the page date.jsp:

<P><jsp:include page="date.jsp" flush="true" />

</BODY>
</HTML>
```

The output of this page is fairly simple (see Figure 3–1).

What is interesting is the source of the page. Notice that everything on the page was included, even the HTML open and close tags. It is also important to note that it was the output of the date.jsp page that was inserted into the page, not the source of the date.jsp page. The include action is "dumb" in the sense

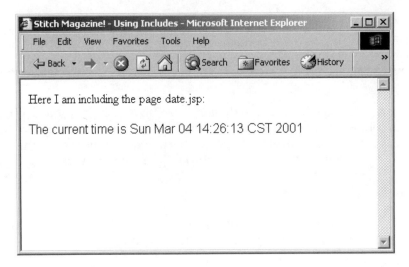

FIGURE 3–1 Output of `include.jsp`

that it does not parse the contents of the page but inserts them "as-is". This means that the page was retrieved like a normal client. The JSP elements on `date.jsp` were processed before being inserted into `include.jsp` (see Figure 3–2).

`<jsp:forward>`

The `forward` action terminates the action of the current page and forwards the request to another resource, such as a static page, another JSP page, or a Java servlet. A JSP page or servlet must be in the same context. Exactly what is forwarded is determined by the value of the `page` implicit object.

The `forward` action is similar to the HTTP status code 302, where a server tells the browser to forward to a new URL. It is different in the fact that the URL specified must reside on the same server. It is also different in that the browser typically displays the same URL as the original request. In essence, a `forward` action receives a request, forwards it to the new URL, receives the response, and then returns it to the client. The client itself never has an indication that there was a `forward` action, or that the page it requested received its content from another resource.

The `forward` action has only one parameter: `page`. Similar to the `include` action, the value of the `page` attribute must be a relative URL on the same Web server.

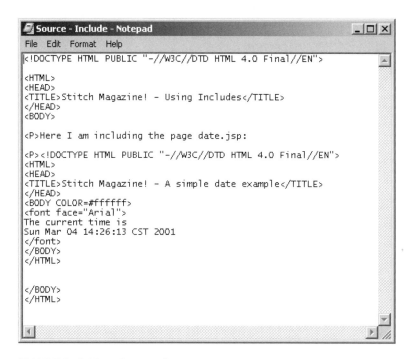

FIGURE 3–2 View Source of `include.jsp`

Script 3.2
`forward.jsp` on the Server

```
<!DOCTYPE HTML PUBLIC "-//W3C//DTD HTML 4.0 Final//EN">

<HTML>
<HEAD>
<TITLE>Stitch Magazine! - Using a Forward</TITLE>
</HEAD>
<BODY>

<jsp:forward page="date.jsp" />

</BODY>
</HTML>
```

Again, the same `date.jsp` is being used, although this time it is forwarded by `forward.jsp`. The output of the page (Figure 3–3) looks almost exactly the same as Figure 3–1. The URL would still show `forward.jsp`. The user has no idea that the page that was really retrieved was `date.jsp`.

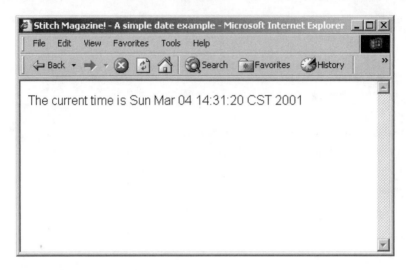

FIGURE 3–3 Output of `forward.jsp`

Figure 3–3 shows the output of `forward.jsp`. Now take a look at the source of this page (Figure 3–4).

The important thing to notice is that all of the data before and after the `forward` action was discarded. This means that the buffer for the actual `forward.jsp` was discarded. In the event that an original page is not buffered, and there was data sent to it, an exception would be raised.

```
<!DOCTYPE HTML PUBLIC "-//W3C//DTD HTML 4.0 Final//EN">
<HTML>
<HEAD>
<TITLE>Stitch Magazine! - A simple date example</TITLE>
</HEAD>
<BODY COLOR=#ffffff>
<font face="Arial">
The current time is
Sun Mar 04 14:31:20 CST 2001
</font>
</BODY>
</HTML>
```

FIGURE 3–4 View Source of `forward.jsp`

With the JSP 1.1 specification, an optional `param` attribute can specify request parameters to be sent to the resource.

```
<jsp:forward page="/authenticate/verify.jsp">
    <jsp:param name="pass" value="dhThs&7" />
</jsp:forward>
```

`<jsp:plugin>`

The `plugin` action is used to insert Java components into JSP. It determines the type of browser and inserts the `<object>` or `<embed>` tags as needed. If the needed plugin is not present, it downloads the plugin and then executes the Java component. The Java component can be either an applet or a JavaBean.

It is important to note that any component specified by the plugin URL must be downloaded to the browser and executed on the client. Thus, JavaBeans used with the `plugin` action are run on the client's Java Runtime Environment (JRE), while JavaBeans used with the `useBean` action are executed on the server.

The `plugin` action has several attributes that correspond to common HTML tags used to format Java components (see Table 3–7). The `param` element can also be used to send parameters to the applet or bean. A new element, the `fallback` element, can be used to specify an error string to be sent to the user in case the component fails. How this message is sent to the client is left up to the specific JSP engine implementation. Possibly, an error dialog is raised. The component fails if either the browser is not compatible with the `<object>` or `<embed>` tags or if the component could not be successfully started.

TABLE 3–7 `<jsp:plugin>` Attributes

type	The type of component specified; either Java-Bean or applet.
jrevision	Identifies the version of the JRE necessary for the component. The default value is "1.1" with JSP specifications 1.0 and 1.1. With the JSP 1.2 specification, it is "1.2".
iepluginurl	The URL where the appropriate Java plugin can be found for Microsoft Internet Explorer. The default value is dependent on the JSP engine implementation.
nspluginurl	The URL where the appropriate Java plugin can be found for Netscape Navigator. The default value is dependent on the JSP engine implementation.

`code, align, archive, height, hspace, name, vspace, title,` **and** `width`	These attributes are defined by the HTML specification and apply to the `codebase` that corresponds to the HTML tags for the appropriate browser.

The `jrevision` attribute allows a minimum level of Java specification necessary to run the component. With the `iepluginurl` and `nspluginurl` attributes, a URL pointing to the appropriate plugin can be specified.

Table 3–7 lists the attributes of the `plugin` action. Here is an example `plugin` action using several different features:

```
<jsp:plugin type="applet" code="JavaCharter.class" codebase="/java"
    vspace="0" hspace="0" width="60" height="80" jrevision="1.2" >
  <jsp:param name="ChartType" value="Bar" />
  <jsp:fallback> Unable to initialize Java Plugin </jsp:fallback>
</jsp:plugin>
```

◆ 3.3 Recap

JSP action elements add powerful functionality to JSP pages. The JavaBean actions allow powerful Java applications written in the JavaBean format to be executed from JSP. Resource actions allow resources such as page includes, page forwards, and client-side objects to be accessible from within a JSP page.

While the JSP actions are concerned with accessing objects outside of the JSP page, the JSP directives are utilized for describing and formatting the JSP page and resulting Java servlet. Chapter 4 covers directives.

◆ 3.4 Advanced Project

Create a Web portal framework out of a few JSP pages and the `forward` and `include` actions. Make the page dynamic, so that different pages "included" within the portal are automatically generated. In other words, replace client-side frame functionality with JSP code.

For portal "pieces," utilize the preceding calendar and date examples, or grab data from other sites on the Internet.

4 Directives

IN THIS CHAPTER

- Directive Syntax
- The page Directive
- The include Directive
- The taglib Directive
- Recap

JSP directives have a very simple purpose: to send messages to the JSP engine. They do not contain business logic. They do not modify the output stream. They simply tell the JSP engine how the JSP page should be compiled. While this purpose is straightforward, understanding directives is somewhat complex. As directives modify how a JSP page is compiled, understanding how they work needs an understanding of the JSP engine. This includes understanding the implicit JSP objects, page scope, error handling, and page buffering.

◆ 4.1 Directive Syntax

JSP Syntax:

```
<%@ directive_name %>
```

XML Syntax:

```
<jsp:directive.directive_name />
```

The syntax for directive elements, both JSP and XML versions, is very different for both action and scripting element tags. The JSP syntax for directive elements begins with a standard JSP open tag and an @ symbol (`<%@`). Similar to action tags, it takes attribute/value pairs. For example:

```
<%@ include file="mypage.html" %>
```

The XML syntax is specific to the directive that is being used. In the JSP 1.0 specification, there are two directives: `page` and `include`. The JSP 1.1 specification adds the `taglib` directive. The XML versions of the `page` and `include` directives are as follows:

```
<jsp:directive.page attribute="value" . . . />
<jsp:directive.include file="value"/>
```

The `taglib` directive's XML syntax is different because its purpose is to define new elements. Instead of being a part of the JSP XML syntax, it extends the JSP XML syntax.

◆ 4.2 The `page` Directive

The `page` directive allows several different page-specific attributes to be set. It directly influences how the Java program created from the JSP page is formed. The JSP page, including any JSP pages included with the `include` directive, can have any number of `page` directives. There must not be more than one instance of each attribute/value pair with the single exception of the `import` attribute. Multiple `import` attribute pairs are cumulative.

`page` directives always begin with the standard JSP open tag followed by an @ symbol and the key word `page` (`<%@ page`). Here are a couple of example `page` directives:

```
<%@ page import="java.util.Calendar" %>
```

The above `page` directive imports the `java.utilCalendar` class. This next example sets the scripting language to `java` and the page buffer to `32k`:

```
<%@ page language="java" buffer="32k" %>
```

It is important to note that the `page` directive is able to affect the overall construction of the Java program that results from the JSP page. For example, the `import` attribute adds to the `import` statements in the Java program, which are location-dependent. This means that within the JSP page, they are location-independent. Wherever the page directive is located, it affects the page as a whole.

4.2.1 The buffer and autoFlush Attributes

The buffer attribute determines whether the JSP page will be buffered, and the buffer size, if it is to be buffered. By default, the page buffer is at least 8K, but the actual value is dependent on the specific JSP engine used. If "none" is specified, the page is not buffered at all, and all output is written directly to a PrintWriter of the ServletResponse object. If a size is specified, such as 16K, then the output is buffered to a JspWriter object with a buffer no less than the size specified.

The buffer attribute is closely tied to the autoFlush attribute. The autoFlush attribute determines the page's behavior when the page buffer is full or exceeded. By default, autoFlush is set to "true". This means that the buffered output is automatically flushed when the buffer is full. By setting the autoFlush attribute to "false", the JSP engine is instructed to raise an exception if the buffer is exceeded.

The forward action can be influenced by the buffer attribute. With a buffer attribute set to "none", a JSP page can have no output before the forward action is encountered or an exception will be raised. Similarly, if the buffer is filled before a forward action is reached, whether or not autoFlush is set, an exception will occur.

4.2.2 The contentType Attribute

The contentType attribute is used to define the encoding for the JSP page in the response, as well as the MIME type of the response. The contentType attribute can take two different types of values. One form simply specifies the MIME type, and is in the form of "*TYPE*". Additionally, a character set can be set, changing the form of the value to "*TYPE*; charset=*CHARSET*". By default, the MIME type or "*TYPE*" value is "text/html" and the character set is ISO-8859-1 (also known as latin-1).

The contentType attribute can be useful in debugging. By setting the value to "text/plain", the output of the JSP file can be seen as source, instead of HTML.

4.2.3 The errorPage and isErrorPage Attributes

The errorPage attribute specifies a URL for forwarding exceptions. In the event an exception is thrown in the current JSP page, but not caught, the thrown exception is forwarded to the specified URL. Currently, the URL specified must be a JSP page, although this may change in later specifications.

The exception is forwarded by saving the object reference on the common `ServletRequest` object by using its `setAttribute()` method. The name used is `javax.Servlet.jsp.jspException`.

If the current JSP page has `buffer="none"` or the buffer has been flushed before the exception is caught, the attempt to forward the exception to the `errorPage` URL might fail. This is similar to the problem of using a `forward` action after the buffer has been flushed, as discussed above.

The JSP page sent an exception by means of an `errorPage` attribute must have the `page` attribute of `isErrorPage` set to "`true`". By default, this attribute is set to "`false`". If "`true`," an explicit scripting variable called `exception` is created and referenced to the `Throwable` error object from the source JSP page.

ESSENTIAL NOTE: ERRORS AND EXCEPTIONS

There are two different types of errors that can occur for any given JSP page. The difference between the two different types of errors is when they occur in the phase or life cycle of the JSP page.

The first type of error is referred to as a translation-time or compile-time error. This type of error occurs the first time the JSP page receives a client request, but before a response is sent. The first time a JSP page is requested, the JSP engine must parse the JSP page and create a Java servlet source file for the JSP page. It then must successfully compile the Java servlet into a Java class file. Any error occurring during this phase is referred to as a translation-time error, as the error is raised as the JSP source is translated into a Java class file. These errors are not caught by the `errorPage` attribute of the `page` directive, as the Java program itself is not operational. Most occurrences of translation-time errors return an HTTP status code of 500 to the client, signifying an unspecified server problem. Translation-time errors are analogous to fatal errors received when compiling a Java source file.

The second type of error is referred to as a client-request or request-time error. This is an error that occurs as a client sends a request to the Java class file and a response is sent back to the client. A common cause of a request-time error is receiving incorrect request (GET or POST) data. Request-time errors can be caught by the `errorPage` attribute of the `page` directive, as well as by `catch` statements within valid JSP tags. Request-time errors are analogous to exceptions raised when executing a Java class file.

4.2.4 *The* extends *Attribute*

The extends attribute allows the JSP author to specify the super-class from which the current JSP page is transformed. In general, it is recommended that the extends attribute be used as little as possible. If no extends attribute is specified, the JSP container can utilize special superclasses to improve JSP speed.

With the JSP 1.1 specification and above, JSP authors have the ability to create new objects with the taglib directive. This gives access to new objects and classes, while allowing the JSP container to utilize its own specialized superclasses.

4.2.5 *The* import *Attribute*

The import attribute allows types to be made available to the Java environment. Multiple values can be specified, separated by commas. The import attribute can also be specified more than once in a JSP page or in pages included in an include directive.

By default, the java.lang.*, javax.Servlet.*, javax. Servlet.jsp.*, and javax.Servlet.http.* packages are im-ported. It is important to note that the import attribute is only available when the language attribute is set to "java".

4.2.6 *The* info *Attribute*

The info attribute simply defines a String that is incorporated into the JSP page. This String can then be obtained by using the page's servlet.getServletInfo() method.

4.2.7 *The* isThreadSafe *Attribute*

The isThreadSafe attribute specifies the thread safety of the JSP page. By default, this attribute is "true". A "true" value tells the JSP engine that it is safe to dispatch multiple client requests to this page at the same time. With a value of "false", the JSP en-gine is required to process each page request one at a time in the order in which they were received.

It is important to note that even with a value of "false", the JSP page must still deal with synchronization issues, espe-cially when concerning the HttpSession and ServletContect objects.

4.2.8 *The* language *Attribute*

The language attribute of the page directive specifies the script-ing language utilized within the JSP page. This includes all scriptlets, declarations, and expressions, as well as any pages included with the `include` directive. The default value is "`java`", and most JSP engines currently only support Java as the scripting language.

Any scripting language utilized in a JSP page has to meet certain conditions. First of all, it must conform to the JRE. Next, it must expose certain parts of Java to the JSP page, including the Java object model, as well as the implicit variables, JavaBean properties, and public methods used in the JSP specification.

4.2.9 The *session* Attribute

The `session` attribute indicates whether or not the current JSP page should participate in an HTTP session. The default value is "`true`". When "`true`", a variable named "`session`" is created with a type of `javax.Servlet.HttpSession`. With a value of "`false`", there is no "`session`" variable created.

HTTP sessions allow information about a particular client to be tracked between requests. Sessions will be discussed thoroughly in future chapters.

◆ 4.3　The `include` Directive

The `include` directive allows data from an external URL to be inserted into the current JSP page. Unlike the `page` directive, the `include` directive is position-dependent. Wherever the `include` directive is placed on the page is where the data will be inserted.

The `include` directive inserts the data from the external URL at translation-time. This means that the data is included in the current JSP page before it is compiled. Any JSP tags within the external URL will be processed as part of the current page. This means that the external resource can affect the current page's HTTP headers. A drawback is that if the external resource changes, the current page has no way of being notified. To see any changes in the external URL, the current page would have to be recompiled. Another drawback is that the external resource cannot be specified at request time, as it is already compiled into the code.

The `include` directive takes only one attribute, `file`, which is required. The following are two examples of the `include` directive:

```
<%@ include file="footer.jsp" %>

<%@ include file="/products/examples/listing.html" %>
```

4.3.1 The `include` Action vs. the `include` Directive

The `include` directive is very similar to the `include` action. Both take data from an external URL and insert it into the current page. When and how they insert the data create very important differences between the tags.

The `include` action inserts the data from the external URL at request-time. What actually happens is that the current JSP page halts and flushes any buffers. It then calls the external URL and inserts the output of the URL into the output stream. After the external page is complete it resumes processing the original JSP page.

By contrast, the `include` directive inserts the raw data from a URL into the page before it has been compiled. When this happens, a preprocessing step occurs that gathers the appropriate data and inserts the information into a temporary version of the page, then the temporary page is compiled. Since the inserted code is really part of the same JSP page, it can take advantage of other parts of the page or change how the page behaves (such as changing the HTTP headers).

Each approach has powerful and distinct advantages and disadvantages that are outlined in Table 4–1

TABLE 4–1 include Action vs. include Directive

	Directive	Action
Syntax	<%@ include ... %>	<jsp:include ... >
Attribute	file='...'	page='...'
Dynamic	Not allowed	Allowed
		(e.g., page="<%=foo%>")
Processed at	Translation-time	Request-time
Scope	Can affect the rest of the page	Cannot affect other parts of the page
Can Contain HTTP Headers?	Yes	No

ESSENTIAL NOTE: INCLUDES AS COMPONENTS

Using either the `include` action or the `include` directive provides a simple and effective way of creating modular components.

By creating a wrapper page that includes the components it needs, a large and complex page can be broken into logic blocks.

Other pages can then reuse the same blocks by including the same files and have the same results. In addition, changing the source of a single block will change each page equally.

◆ 4.4 The `taglib` Directive

The `taglib` directive is available in the JSP 1.1 specification and above. It specifies a tag library by which the standard set of JSP tags can be extended. The `taglib` directive accomplishes three tasks. First, it tells the JSP engine that this JSP page uses a tag library. This significantly affects the structure of the underlying Java program. Second, it specifies a URI that points to a special JAR file containing a tag library descriptor (TLD). The TLD describes the semantics of the new tag library. Finally, the `taglib` directive specifies a tag prefix that will be used to uniquely distinguish the new tags.

There are only two `taglib` attributes and they are both required: `uri` is set to the path of the tag library for the selected set of tags, while `prefix` represents the handle that will represent the library within the page. For example:

```
<%@ taglib
uri="http://www.javadesktop.com/taglib/sample.jar"
    prefix="sample" %>
<sample:tagAction> This is an example </sample:tagAction>
```

In the above example, the `taglib` directive points to a JAR file called `sampletags.jar`. It gives the new set of tags the prefix `sample`. Once the new tag library is referenced, an action from the tag library can be used. The example calls an action called `tagAction` from the tag library.

◆ 4.5 Recap

It should be obvious that JSP directives go a step beyond scripting elements to give the JSP author tools to make dynamic Web pages into Web applications. Now that the JSP directives have been discussed, the next chapter will take a look under the hood of JSP pages to explore their relationship with Java servlets.

5 The JSP Engine

IN THIS CHAPTER

- Behind the Scenes
- Multithreading and Persistence
- Implicit Objects
- The JSP Life Cycle
- JSP Compiled
- Recap

The previous chapters addressed the background, syntax, and elements of JSP. Until this point, many of the technical details of how the JSP engine works have been glossed over or avoided entirely. Developing good JSP applications involves at least a basic understanding of how the JSP engine works.

◆ 5.1 Behind the Scenes

When the JSP engine receives a request for a page, it converts both static data and dynamic elements of a JSP page into Java code fragments. This translation is actually fairly straightforward.

The dynamic data elements contained within the JSP elements are already Java code, so these fragments can be used without modification. The static data gets wrapped up into `println()` methods. These Java code fragments are then sequentially put into a special wrapper class.

The JSP wrapper is created automatically by the JSP engine and handles most of the work involved in supporting JSP without the author's involvement. The wrapper usually extends the `javax.servlet.Servlet` class, which means that JSP actually get converted into a special form of Java servlet code. In many ways, JSP could be considered a macro language for creating Java servlets; JSP essentially provide a page-centric interface into the Java Servlet API.

The source code is then compiled into a fully functioning Java servlet. This new servlet created by the JSP engine deals with basic exception handling, I/O, threading, and a number of other network and protocol-related tasks. It is actually this newly generated servlet that handles requests and generates output to the client requesting the JSP page.

5.1.1 Recompiling

The JSP engine could have been designed to recompile each page when a new request is received. Each request would generate its own servlet to process the response. Fortunately, JSP takes a more efficient approach.

JSP pages and Java servlets create an instance once per page, rather than once per request. When a new request is received, it simply creates a thread within the already generated servlet. This means that the first request to a JSP page will generate a new servlet, but subsequent requests will simply reuse the servlet from the initial request.

ESSENTIAL NOTE: DELAY ON FIRST REQUEST
When a JSP page is first run through the JSP engine, there may be a noticeable delay in receiving a response. These delays occur because the JSP engine needs to convert the JSP into Java code, compile it, and initialize it before responding to the first request.

Subsequent requests gain the advantage of using the already compiled servlet. Requests after the initial request should process significantly faster.

There are specific occurrences that can instruct the JSP engine when to recompile a JSP page. To manage this, the JSP engine keeps a record of the JSP page source code and recompiles the page when the source code has been modified. Different implementations of JSP have different rules for when to compile, but all engines are required to recompile when the JSP source code changes.

Keep in mind that external resources to a JSP page, such as a JavaBean or an included JSP page, may not cause the page to re-compile. Again, different JSP engines will have different rules on how and when to recompile a page.

ESSENTIAL NOTE: THE PRECOMPILE PROTOCOL
As of JSP 1.1, a means of precompiling JSP pages is defined in the specification. To precompile a specific JSP page, an HTTP request to the JSP page must be made with the `jsp_precompile` parameter set.

For example, entering the URL `http://www.javadesktop.com/jsp/catalog.jsp?jsp_precompile="true"` should compile this JSP, if it has not already been compiled or the JSP source code changed.

5.1.2 The Servlet–JSP Relationship

Because JSP pages are transformed into Java servlets, JSP displays many of the same behaviors as Java servlets. JSP inherits both advantages and disadvantages from Java servlets.

Java servlets work by creating a single persistent application running in the JVM. New requests are actually handled by run-ning a new thread through this persistent application. Each re-quest to a JSP page is really a new thread in the corresponding Java servlet.

The Java servlet also provides the JSP developer with several built-in methods and objects. These provide a direct interface into the behavior of the servlet and the JSP engine.

◆ 5.2 Multithreading and Persistence

JSP inherits multithreading and persistence from Java servlets. Being persistent allows objects to be instantiated when the servlet is first created, so the physical memory footprint of the JSP servlet remains fairly constant between requests. Variables can be cre-ated in persistent space to allow the servlet to perform caching, session tracking, and other functions not normally available in a stateless environment.

The JSP author is insulated from many of the issues involved with threaded programming. The JSP engine handles most of the work involved in creating, destroying, and managing threads. This frees the JSP author from many of the burdens of multi-threaded programming. However, the JSP author needs to be aware of several aspects of multithreaded programming that affect JSP pages.

Threads can inadvertently cause harm to other threads. In these situations the JSP programmer needs to understand when and how to protect his or her pages from threading.

5.2.1 Persistence

Because a servlet is created once and remains running as a constant instance, it allows persistent variables and objects to be created. Persistent variables and objects are shared between all threads of a single servlet. Changes to these persistent objects are reflected in all threads.

From the perspective of the JSP author, all objects and variables created within declaration tags (<%!...%>) are persistent. Variables and objects created within a thread are not persistent. Code inside of a scriptlet, expression or in action tags will be run within the new request thread; therefore, it will not create persistent variables or objects.

Having persistent objects allows the author to keep track of data between page requests. This allows in-memory objects to be used for caching, counters, session data, database connection pooling, and many other useful tasks.

Script 5.1 shows a counter that uses persistent variables. When the page is first loaded, the variable `counter` is created. Since the servlet remains running in memory, the variable will remain until the servlet is restarted. Each time the page is requested, the variable `counter` is incremented and displayed to the requestor. Each user should see a page count that is one higher than the last time the page was accessed.

Script 5.1
`counter.jsp`

```
<!DOCTYPE HTML PUBLIC "-//W3C//DTD HTML 4.0 Final//EN">

<%!
  int counter;
%>

<HTML>

<STYLE>
.pageFooter {
  position: absolute; top: 590px;
  font-family: Arial, Helvetica, sans-serif;
```

```
    font-size: 8pt; text-align: right;
}
</STYLE>

<BODY>
<DIV CLASS="pageFooter">
This page has been accessed
<% counter++;
   out.print(counter);
 %>
times since last restarted.
</DIV>
</BODY>

</HTML>
```

5.2.2 The Dangers of Threads

Unfortunately, object persistence also presents some potentially significant problems. To avoid these problems, the JSP author needs to understand and steer away from these dangers.

The same factors that make persistence useful can also create a significant problem called a *race condition*. A race condition occurs when one thread is preparing to use data and a second thread modifies the data before the first thread has finished using the data.

Consider the above example (Script 5.1) with two threads running. Take careful note of the value of the counter variable.

Thread 1 – User A requests the page.
Thread 2 – User B requests the page.
Thread 1 – counter increases by one.
Thread 2 – counter increases by one.
Thread 1 – counter is displayed for User A.
Thread 2 – counter is displayed for User B.

In this situation, User A is actually viewing information that was intended for User B. This is obviously not the expected result.

The problems caused by the above example are fairly trivial, User A simply sees an incorrect page count. Race conditions can just as easily result in very significant problems. Imagine if race condition occurred while billing a user for an online order.

It is good programming practice to resolve all race conditions, whether they appear trivial or not. Threads do not flow in a predictable order, so the results of a race condition may appear erratic. Race conditions can be particularly difficult to spot and can turn from trivial to significant with very minor changes to the processing algorithms.

5.2.3 Thread Safety

In considering thread safety, it is important to first acknowledge that threading is a significant benefit to performance. Thread safety is almost always achieved by "disabling" threading for some portion of the code.

It is also important to understand that race conditions only occur with persistent variables. If all the variables and objects used by an application are created by threads, then there will be no race conditions. In these cases, threading problems are not going to occur.

SingleThreadModel

The simplest method for gaining thread safety is also the least efficient. This is achieved by simply turning off threading for the entire page. Turning off threading is a poor option and should be avoided in most situations because it avoids potential problems by sacrificing many advantages.

JSP provides a means to turn off threading through the `page` directive attribute `isThreadSafe='false'`. This will force the page to be created under the `SingleThreadModel`, which allows only one request to be handled by the page at any time.

This option is still not 100% effective. Variables created in the `session` or `application` scope may still be affected by multiple instances.

synchronized()

A more practical and efficient manner of protecting variables from race conditions is to use Java's synchronized interface. This interface imposes a locking mechanism that allows only one thread at a time to process a particular block of code.

Entire methods can be synchronized and protected from race conditions by using the `synchronized` keyword in the methods signature. This will protect all persistent variables accessed within the method. In this case, only one thread can access the method at a time.

Blocks of code can also be synchronized by wrapping the code in a `synchronized()` block. In this case, an argument is expected, which should represent the object to be locked.

ESSENTIAL NOTE: SYNCHRONIZED FLAG

Any object derived from `java.lang.Object` can be used as the argument to the synchronized block. Every object has a special "lock flag" that is used by `synchronized()` to manage threading (`synchronized()` replaces both mutex and semaphore use in C programming). Primitive types in Java do not have this flag and therefore cannot be used as a lock for a synchronized block.

In creating a synchronized block, it is usually most efficient to use the object which most closely represents the data to be synchronized. For example, if a synchronized block is being written that modifies and writes the `foo` object to disk, it is best to use `synchronized(foo)`. Of course, the `this` or `page` object can always be used, but that can create bottlenecks by locking the entire page each time the synchronized block is run.

Script 5.2 shows a new example of the counter page that uses a synchronized block. In this new example, the two lines of code are grouped together within the synchronized block. Only one thread is able to process the block at any given time. Each thread will lock the page object, increment the variable, display the variable, and then unlock the page object.

Script 5.2
counter2.jsp

```
<!DOCTYPE HTML PUBLIC "-//W3C//DTD HTML 4.0 Final//EN">

<%!
  int counter;
%>

<HTML>

<STYLE>
.pageFooter {
  position: absolute; top: 590px;
  font-family: Arial, Helvetica, sans-serif;
  font-size: 8pt; text-align: right;
}
</STYLE>

<BODY>
<DIV CLASS="pageFooter">
This page has been accessed
```

```
<% synchronized (page) {
    counter++;
    out.print(counter);
  }
%>
times since last restarted.
</DIV>
</BODY>

</HTML>
```

◆ 5.3 Implicit Objects

The servlet also creates several objects to be used by the JSP engine. Many of these objects are exposed to the JSP developer and can be called directly without being explicitly declared.

5.3.1 The `out` Object

The `out` object is the major function of JSP to describe data being sent to an output stream in response to a client request. This output stream is exposed to the JSP author through the implicit `out` object.

The `out` object is an instantiation of a `javax.servlet.jsp.JspWriter` object. This object may represent a direct reference to the output stream, a filtered stream, or a nested `JspWriter` from another JSP page. Output should never be sent directly to the output stream, because there may be several output streams during the life cycle of the JSP.

The initial `JspWriter` object is instantiated differently depending on whether the page is buffered or not. By default, every JSP page has buffering turned on, which almost always improves performance. Buffering can be easily turned off by using the `buffered='false'` attribute of the `page` directive.

A buffered `out` object collects and sends data in blocks, typically providing the best total throughput. With buffering, the `PrintWriter` is created when the first block is sent, actually the first time that `flush()` is called.

With unbuffered output, the `PrintWriter` object will be immediately created and referenced to the `out` object. In this situation, data sent to the `out` object is immediately sent to the output stream. The `PrintWriter` will be created using the default settings and header information determined by the server.

ESSENTIAL NOTE: HTTP HEADERS AND BUFFERING

HTTP uses response headers to both describe the server and define certain aspects of the data begin sent to the client. This might include the MIME content type of the page, new cookies, a forwarding URL, or other HTTP "actions.

JSP allows the author to change aspects of the response headers right up until the `OutputStream` is created. Once the `OutputStream` is established, the header information cannot be modified as it has already been sent to the client.

In the case of a buffered `out` object, the `OutputStream` is not established until the first time the buffer is flushed. When the buffer gets flushed depends largely on the `autoFlush` and `bufferSize` attributes of the `page` directive. It is usually best to set the header information before anything is sent to the `out` object.

It is very difficult to set page headers with an unbuffered `out` object. When an unbuffered page is created, the `OutputStream` is established almost immediately.

The sending of headers after the `OutputStream` has been established can result in a number of unexpected behaviors. Some headers will simply be ignored; others may generate exceptions such as `IllegalStateException`.

The `JspWriter` object contains most of the same methods as the `java.io.PrintWriter` class. However, `JspWriter` has some additional methods designed to deal with buffering. Unlike the `PrintWriter` object, `JspWriter` throws `IOExceptions`. In JSP, these exceptions need to be explicitly caught and dealt with.

ESSENTIAL NOTE: `autoFlush()`

The default behavior of buffering in JSP is to automatically flush the buffer when it becomes full. However, there are cases where a JSP page is actually talking directly to another application. In these cases the desired behavior might be to throw an exception if the buffer size is exceeded.

Setting the `autoFlush='false'` attribute of the `page` directive will cause a buffer overflow to throw an exception.

5.3.2 The `request` Object

Each time a client requests a page, the JSP engine creates a new object to represent that request. This new object is an instance of `javax.servlet.http.HttpServletRequest` and is given parameters describing the request. This object is exposed to the JSP author through the `request` object.

Through the `request` object, the JSP page is able to react to input received from the client. Request parameters are stored in special name/value pairs, which can be retrieved using the `request.getParameter(name)` method.

The `request` object also provides methods to retrieve header information and cookie data. It also provides the means to identify both the client and the server, as seen previously.

The `request` object is inherently limited to the request scope. Regardless of how the `page` directives have set the scope of the page, this object will always be recreated with each request. For each separate request from a client, there will be a corresponding `request` object.

5.3.3 The `response` Object

Just as the server creates the `request` object, it also creates an object to represent the response to the client. The object is an instance of `javax.servlet.http.HttpServletResponse` and is exposed to the JSP author as the `response` object.

The `response` object deals with the stream of data back to the client. The `out` object is very closely related to the `response` object. The `response` object also defines the interfaces that deal with creating new HTTP headers. Through this object, the JSP author can add new cookies or date stamps, change the MIME content type of the page, or start "server push" methods. The `response` object also contains enough information on the HTTP protocols to be able to return HTTP status codes, such as forcing page redirects.

5.3.4 The `pageContext` Object

The `pageContext` object is used to represent the entire JSP page. It is intended as a means to access information about the page while avoiding most of the implementation details.

This object stores references to the `request` and `response` objects for each request. The `application`, `config`, `session`, and `out` objects are derived by accessing attributes of this object. The `pageContext` object also contains information about the directives issued to the JSP page, including buffering information, the errorPageURL, and page scope.

But the pageContext object does more than just act as a data repository. It is this object that manages nested JSP pages, performing most of the work involved with the forward and include actions. The pageContext object also handles uncaught exceptions.

From the perspective of the JSP author, this object is useful in deriving information about the current JSP page's environment. This can be particularly useful in creating components where behavior may be different based on the JSP page directives.

5.3.5 The *session* Object

The session object is used to track information about a particular client while using stateless connection protocols, such as HTTP. Sessions can be used to store arbitrary information between client requests.

Each session should correspond to only one client and can exist throughout multiple requests. Sessions are often tracked by URL rewriting or cookies, but the method for tracking the requesting client is not important to the session object.

The session object is an instance of javax.servlet.http. HttpSession and behaves exactly the same way that session objects behave under Java servlets.

The session object and its methods will be discussed in Chapter 7, "Tracking Sessions."

5.3.6 The *application* Object

The application object is a direct wrapper around the ServletContext object for the generated servlet. It has the same methods and interfaces that the ServletContext object does in programming Java servlets.

This object is a representation of the JSP page through its entire life cycle. This object is created when the JSP page is initialized, and will be removed when the JSP page is removed by the destroy() method, the JSP page is being recompiled, or the JVM crashes. Information stored in this object remains available to any object used within the JSP page.

The application object also provides a means for JSP to communicate back to the server in a way that does not involve "requests." This can be useful for finding out information about the MIME type of a file, sending log information directly out to the server's log, or communicating with other servers.

5.3.7 *The* `config` *Object*

The `config` object is an instantiation of `javax.servlet.Servlet-Config`. This object is a direct wrapper around the `ServletConfig` object for the generated servlet. It has the same methods and interfaces that the `ServletConfig` object does in programming Java servlets.

This object allows the JSP author access to the initialization parameters for the servlet or JSP engine. This can be useful in getting standard global information, such as paths or file locations.

5.3.8 *The* `page` *Object*

This object is an actual reference to the instance of the page. It can be thought of as an object that represents the entire JSP page.

When the JSP page is first instantiated, the `page` object is created by obtaining a reference to the `this` object. So, the `page` object is really a direct synonym for the `this` object.

However, during life cycle of the JSP page, the `this` object may not refer to the page itself. Within the context of the JSP page, the `page` object will remain constant and will always represent the entire JSP page.

5.3.9 *The* `exception` *Object*

The error handling methods described in Chapter 3 utilize this object. It is available only when the previous JSP page throws an uncaught exception and the `<%@ page errorpage="..." %>` tag was used.

The `exception` object is a wrapper containing the exception thrown from the previous page. It is typically used to generate an appropriate response to the error condition.

◆ 5.4 The JSP Life Cycle

The JSP engine uses three methods to manage the life cycle of a JSP page and its generated servlet. The heart of a JSP page is processed using a generated method called `_jspService`. This is created and managed by the JSP engine itself. `_jspService` should never be managed by the JSP author; doing so could cause disastrous results. The `_jspService` method represents the bulk of the JSP page, handling all requests and responses. In fact, new threads effectively call the `_jspService` method.

ESSENTIAL NOTE: RESERVED NAMES
The JSP specification specifically reserves the methods and variables
that begin with `jsp`, `_jsp`, `jspx`, and `_jspx`. Methods and variables
with these names may be accessible to the JSP author; however, new
methods and variables should not be created. The JSP engine expects
to have control over these methods and variables, so changing them
or creating new ones may result in erratic behavior.

Two other methods, `jspInit()` and `jspDestroy()`, are designed to be overridden by the JSP author. In fact, these methods
do not exist unless specifically created by the JSP author. They
play a special role in managing the life cycle of a JSP page.

5.4.1 jspInit()

Method Signature:

```
void jspInit()
```

`jspInit()` is a method that is run only once when the JSP
page is first requested. `jspInit()`is guaranteed to be completely
processed before any single request is handled. It is effectively the
same as the `init()` method in Java servlets and applets.

`jspInit()` allows the JSP author a means to create or load
objects that may be needed for every request. This can be useful
for loading state information, creating database connection
pools, and any task that only needs to happen once when the JSP
page is first started.

5.4.2 jspDestroy()

Method Signature:

```
void jspDestroy()
```

The server calls the `jspDestroy()` method each time a servlet
is unloaded from the JVM. It is effectively the same as the `de-
stroy()` method in Java servlets and applets.

Unlike `jspInit()`, this method is not guaranteed to execute.
The server will make a best attempt to run the method after each
thread. Since this method occurs at the end of processing, there
are situations, such as the server crashing, where `jspDestroy()`
may not be executed.

`jspDestroy()` allows the JSP author a means to execute code
just before the servlet has finished. This is commonly used to free
up resources or close connections that are still open. It can also

be useful to store state information or other information that should be stored between instances.

5.4.3 JSP Life Cycle Overview

On first request or precompile, `jspInit()` will be called, at which point the page is "running," waiting for requests. Now, `_jspService` handles most transactions, picking up requests, running threads through, and generating responses. Finally, when a signal is received to shut down, the `jspDestroy()` method is called.

THE COUNTER USING `jspInit()` AND `jspDestroy()`

The previous example of a page counter used a variable stored only in the memory of the running servlet. It was never written to disk, so if the JSP page was restarted, the variable would be reset.

The example shown in Script 5.3 recovers the variable by using the `jspInit()` method to load the value of the variable when the page is first started. The example also uses the `jspDestroy()` method to write the value of variable to be recovered the next time the JSP page is restarted.

Script 5.3
counter3.jsp

```
<!DOCTYPE HTML PUBLIC "-//W3C//DTD HTML 4.0 Final//EN">

<%@ page import="java.io.*" %>

<%!
  int counter = 0;

  public void jspInit() {
    try {
      FileInputStream countFile =
                      new FileInputStream ("counter.dat");
      DataInputStream countData =
                      new DataInputStream (countFile);
      counter = countData.readInt();
    }
    catch (FileNotFoundException ignore) {
      // No file indicates a new counter.
    }
    catch (IOException e) {
      e.printStackTrace();
    }
  }
```

```
    public void jspDestroy() {
      try {
        FileOutputStream countFile =
                          new FileOutputStream ("counter.dat");
        DataOutputStream countData =
                          new DataOutputStream (countFile);
        countData.writeInt(counter);
      }
      catch (IOException e) {
        e.printStackTrace();
      }
    }
%>

<HTML>

<STYLE>
.pageFooter {
  position: absolute; top: 590px;
  font-family: Arial, Helvetica, sans-serif;
  font-size: 8pt; text-align: right;
}
</STYLE>

<BODY>
<DIV CLASS="pageFooter">
This page has been accessed
<%
  synchronized(page) {
    counter++;
    out.print(counter);
  }
%>
times.
</DIV>
</BODY>

</HTML>
```

◆ 5.5 JSP Compiled

Many implementations of JSP engines leave the servlet source code that they create in a working directory. Under many engines, this is an option that must be explicitly turned on, but it is usually a trivial task to enable.

Reading through generated source code can be extremely useful in debugging problems that are not readily apparent in the JSP page. In addition, this source code can provide experi-

enced Java developers with additional insight about the inner
workings of the JSP implementation.

Script 5.4 shows the compiled source code from the most re-
cent counter. The source code in this listing was generated from
Apache Jakarta Project's Tomcat v3.1; other JSP engines will
probably produce slightly different results. The source code was
also modified slightly to fit better on the page.

Script 5.4
counter3_jsp.java

```java
import javax.servlet.*;
import javax.servlet.http.*;
import javax.servlet.jsp.*;
import javax.servlet.jsp.tagext.*;
import java.io.PrintWriter;
import java.io.IOException;
import java.io.FileInputStream;
import java.io.ObjectInputStream;
import java.util.Vector;
import org.apache.jasper.runtime.*;
import java.beans.*;
import org.apache.jasper.JasperException;
import java.io.*;

public class _0002fcounter3_0002ejspcounter3_jsp_0
                                extends HttpJspBase {

// begin [file="/counter3.jsp";from=(4,3);to=(35,0)]

    int counter = 0;

    public void jspInit() {
      try {
        FileInputStream countFile =
                        new FileInputStream ("counter.dat");
        DataInputStream countData =
                        new DataInputStream (countFile);
        counter = countData.readInt();
      } catch (FileNotFoundException ignore) {
        // No file indicates a new counter.
      } catch (IOException e) {
        e.printStackTrace();
      }
    }

    public void jspDestroy() {
      try {
        FileOutputStream countFile =
```

```
                       new FileOutputStream ("counter.dat");
      DataOutputStream countData =
                       new DataOutputStream (countFile);
      countData.writeInt(counter);
      } catch (IOException e) {
        e.printStackTrace();
      }
    }
  // end

  static { }

  public _0002fcounter3_0002ejspcounter3_jsp_0( ) { }

  private static boolean _jspx_inited = false;

  public final void _jspx_init() throws JasperException { }

  public void _jspService(HttpServletRequest request,
                          HttpServletResponse response)
                     throws IOException, ServletException {

      JspFactory _jspxFactory = null;
      PageContext pageContext = null;
      HttpSession session = null;
      ServletContext application = null;
      ServletConfig config = null;
      JspWriter out = null;
      Object page = this;
      String  _value = null;
      try {

          if (_jspx_inited == false) {
              _jspx_init();
              _jspx_inited = true;
          }
          _jspxFactory = JspFactory.getDefaultFactory();
          response.setContentType("text/html");
          pageContext = _jspxFactory.getPageContext(this,
                                      request, response,
                                      "", true, 8192, true);

          application = pageContext.getServletContext();
          config = pageContext.getServletConfig();
          session = pageContext.getSession();
          out = pageContext.getOut();

          // begin [file="/counter3.jsp";from=(0,0);to=(2,0)]
          out.write("<!DOCTYPE HTML PUBLIC \"-//W3C//DTD HTML "
+
              "4.0 Final//EN\">\r\n\r\n");
```

```
            // end
            // begin [file="/counter3.jsp";from=(2,30);to=(4,0)]
                out.write("\r\n\r\n");
            // end
            // begin [file="/counter3.jsp";from=(35,2);to=(50,0)]

out.write("\r\n\r\n<HTML>\r\n\r\n\r\n<STYLE>\r\n.pageFooter {\r\n po-
    sition: absolute; top: 590px;\r\n font-family: Arial, Hel-
    vetica, sans-serif; \r\n font-size: 8pt; text-align: right;
    \r\n}\r\n</STYLE>\r\n\r\n\r\n<BODY>\r\n<DIV CLASS=\"page-
Footer\">\r\nThis page has been accessed \r\n");
            // end
            // begin [file="/counter3.jsp";from=(50,2);to=(55,0)]

                    synchronized(page) {
                        counter++;
                        out.print(counter);
                    }
            // end
            // begin [file="/counter3.jsp";from=(55,2);to=(62,0)]
                out.write("
\r\ntimes.\r\n</DIV>\r\n</BODY>\r\n\r\n\r\n</HTML>\r\n\r\n\r\n");
            // end

        } catch (Exception ex) {
            if (out.getBufferSize() != 0)
                out.clear();
            pageContext.handlePageException(ex);
        } finally {
            out.flush();
            _jspxFactory.releasePageContext(pageContext);
        }
    }
}
```

◆ 5.6 Recap

It is important to note that JSP, unlike other server-side scripting languages, creates powerful Java servlet applications. This introduces important concepts such as compiling, multithreading, and persistence to JSP. While it is not completely necessary to understand JSP under the hood, a good background gives the JSP author perspective on the Java servlet that will be created from JSP code.

The next chapter deals with retrieving information from the HTTP browser, and how to tailor dynamic output based on user input.

chapter

6 Retrieving Information

IN THIS CHAPTER

- Request
- The HTTP Request and JSP
- Header Information
- Recap

JSP pages, like most Web application platforms, use HTTP as a transport protocol. To understand how a JSP program changes for different requests, one must understand the Web transaction model, which is built upon the HTTP protocol. The model itself is very simple, and it applies to many different Web programming technologies. A good analogy for the Web transaction model is a math function box. A math function box is a tool used to explain how a mathematical function works (see Figure 6–1). The important thing to understand is that the function box itself never changes. The only reason why an output changes is if an input changes. It is exactly the same with JSP pages. The JSP page itself does not change, but it generates different output based on different input.

This chapter focuses on the input to the JSP page, known as the HTTP request, or simply the request. The next chapter focuses on the HTTP response, or simply the response. By creating a custom response based on the request, the resulting Web page is considered dynamic. The next logical step is to group these dynamic Web pages together for a specific Web client. This grouping is known as a session. A session is a system by which information about a specific client can be stored between each request/response pair. By maintaining a session, Web pages are considered to be interactive. These two characteristics, dynamic content and in-

teractivity, are what distinguish a Web application from a simple Web page.

◆ 6.1 The Request

An HTTP request is a simple data structure. It is composed of a block of text that is separated by newline characters. The first line is the request itself. The request line is made up of three sets of data. The first section is the HTTP request type. Two common types are GET and POST. Next is part of the URL of the document requested, and finally, the version of HTTP. An example request line might be:

```
GET /index.html HTTP/1.0
```

The next sets of lines are called headers. Headers consist of parameter/value pairs separated by a colon. Example headers might be Server: followed by the type of server, or Accept: followed by the different MIME types the client will accept.

Following the request line and header lines of an HTTP request, the client can optionally send a blank line followed by content or "body" data. This is dependent on the type of HTTP request. For example, a GET request does not have any body data after the headers section, but can include specific data within the URL. A POST request can include the same data after a blank line in the HTTP request.

It is important to understand that all of the information about a client comes from the HTTP request. This means information about a client such as browser type or IP address, as well as any data submitted via a form, is included within the HTTP request, in the request line, a header, or content data.

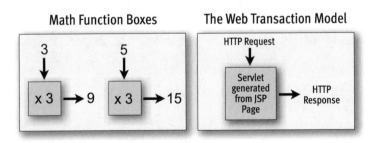

FIGURE 6–1 JSP and Math Function Boxes

◆ 6.2 The HTTP Request and JSP

Because the HTTP request and HTTP response are such a critical part of JSP, they are the two parameters for the Java class generated from any JSP page. The request object is of the type `HttpServletRequest` and is simply named `request`. The authors of the JSP specification provide many different methods for accessing information inside a request, both in raw data format as well as with convenience methods.

Parameters

```
String request.getQueryString()
BufferedReader request.getReader()
ServletInputStream request.getInputStream()
String request.getMethod()
String request.getParameter(String)
Enumeration request.getParameterNames()
String[] request.getParameterValues(String)
```

One of the most common types of data retrieved from a request is referred to as *parameters* in the JSP specification. Most often, this is information sent via a query string in a GET request or form data sent with a POST request. The JSP API specification has two sets of methods for accessing parameter information: getting the information in a "raw" format and allowing the JSP author to process it, and parsing the information for the JSP author in convenience methods.

6.2.1 Raw Parameter Methods

If the author desires, this data is available in its raw format. For GET requests, the `request` object has a method called `getQueryString()`, which returns a `String` containing the text after the question mark in the URL string. For POST requests, it is more complicated, as the content of the POST is basically seen as a file of the MIME type `text/plain`. The request object contains a method called `getReader()`, which returns a `BufferedReader` object containing the POST data.

For other HTTP request types that contain binary content data the `request` object has the `getInputStream()` method, which returns a `ServletInputStream` object containing the attached data. To know which of these methods to use, the `getMethod()` method of the `request` object can be called to determine the HTTP request type, whether it is GET, POST, or any other type supported by HTTP.

It is important to note that getting the data in raw format is usually only the first step. For example, a space character sent from a form using the GET HTTP format will be encoded as a "%20" using URL encoding. To use the query string, the author would first have to decode the string (convert the "%20" back into a space). Parsing parameters from a BufferedReader object from a POST request is even more difficult, as it involves working directly with Java I/O methods.

ESSENTIAL NOTE: UTF-8

UTF-8 actually stands for Universal Character Set Transformation Format 8. UTF-8 is simply a character set that is agreed upon by Web server and browser manufacturers to be the standard for sending and retrieving information in text format. UTF-8 is actually a superset of the Unicode character-encoding standard, with some added benefits. In UTF-8 all ASCII characters are preserved in standard ASCII format. This means that programs that are not Unicode compatible, but are ASCII-aware, can interpret UTF-8-encoded text. This is the case with many operating systems.

6.2.2 Convenience Parameter Methods

Getting parameter data is one of the most common functions in a JSP page, so the JSP specification authors have thoughtfully provided three convenience methods for accessing and utilizing the HTTP request data. Data sent in a GET or POST request is usually in pairs. Thus, the convenience methods work around a name/value paradigm. To this extent, the JSP engine automatically parses the query string or POST content data and inserts the name / value pairs in an array stored within the request object.

The simplest convenience method is the getParameter() method. It takes a string as an argument representing the parameter name and returns a string containing the value of the specified parameter. For example, given the URL http://www.javadesktop.com/prog.jsp?name=bob, if prog.jsp contained the line: <% String val = request.getParameter ("name"); %>, then the text contained within the string val would be "bob". The same would be true if the request was received via a POST request. If the parameter name "name" did not exist at all, a null would be returned.

This works well if the parameter name is known, but what if the names of the parameters sent are unknown? The JSP specification authors provide the `getParameterNames()` function in this situation. `getParameterNames()` returns an `Enumeration` containing the name of each parameter. An `Enumeration` is an object that is very similar to the `Iterator` object in Java 1.2. It contains a list of objects that can be referenced one at a time with the `nextElement()` method. As the elements within an `Enumeration` are stored as `java.lang.Object`, a cast is necessary to assign them to a `String` object. This must be done if they are going to be used to obtain matching values with the `getParameter()` method. With the `getParameterNames()` and `getParameter()` methods used together, all name/value pairs can be displayed.

```
<%
    Enumeration requestNames = request.getParameterNames();
    while (requestNames.hasMoreElements()) {
        String currentName = (String)requestNames.nextElement();
        String currentVal = request.getParameter(currentName);
        out.print(currentName + " = " + currentVal + "<br>");
    }
}
%>
```

There is still one situation where a problem might occur: when two parameters have the same name but different values. Will the `getParameter()` method work if there is more than one value for a given name? In most cases, yes, but this is JSP implementation-dependent. For example, the JSP engine can choose to either return the first or last value corresponding to the parameter name. One popular JSP engine returns a single string that is comma-delimited and contains all of the values.

In any case, the value of the `getParameter()` method is not guaranteed to work the same across all implementations. To solve this problem, there is the `getParameterValues()` method. `getParameterValues()` takes a `String` containing the parameter name just like the `getParameter()` method. It returns a `String` array containing all of the values corresponding to the given name.

Combining all three convenience methods, `getParameter()`, `getParameterNames()`, and `getParameterValues()`, allows all data sent from a POST or GET request to be accessed. Script 6.1 shows a JSP page that uses all three of these methods, as well as the `getMethod()` and `getQueryString()` methods, to retrieve and display all GET and POST data sent.

Script 6.1
parameters.jsp

```
<!DOCTYPE HTML PUBLIC "-//W3C//DTD HTML 4.0 Final//EN">
<%@ page import="java.util.Enumeration" %>

<HTML>
<HEAD>
<TITLE>Stitch Magazine! - Request Info</TITLE>
</HEAD>
<BODY BGCOLOR="white">
<H1> Request Information </H1>
<H2> Request MetaData: </H2>
<FONT SIZE=4>
Request Method: <CODE><%= request.getMethod() %></CODE>
<BR>
Query string: <CODE><%= request.getQueryString() %></CODE>
</FONT>

<H2> Parameter Names and Values: </H2>
<FONT SIZE=4>
<CODE>
<TABLE BORDER=0>
<%
   Enumeration requestNames = request.getParameterNames();
   StringBuffer outPut = new StringBuffer();

   while (requestNames.hasMoreElements()) {

     String     Name = (String)requestNames.nextElement();
     String[] Values = request.getParameterValues(Name);

     for(int count = 0; count < Values.length; count++){
       outPut.append("<TR>")
             .append("<TD>").append(Name).append("</TD>")
             .append("<TD> = </TD>")
             .append("<TD>").append(Values[count])
             .append("</TD>")
             .append("</TR>\n");
       Name = " ";
     }
   }
   out.print(outPut.toString());
%>
</TABLE>
</CODE></FONT>
</BODY>
</HTML>
```

Notice that the code utilizes a StringBuffer object to store the page output instead of concatenating String objects. This is

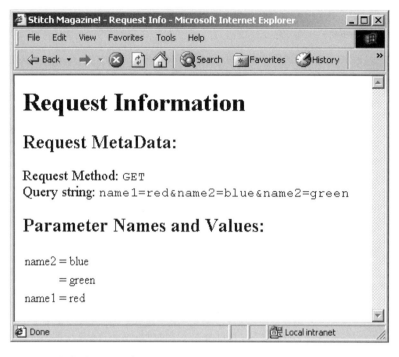

FIGURE 6–2 Output of `parameters.jsp`

much more efficient. With a query string of "?name1=red&name2=blue&name2=green", this page will return a page similar to Figure 6–2.

◆ 6.3 Header Information

```
String request.getHeader(String)
int request.getIntHeader(String)
Date request.getDateHeader(String)
Enumeration request.getHeaderNames()
Enumeration request.getHeaders(String)
String request.getLocale()
Enumeration request.getLocales()
```

In addition to parameter information, the HTTP request may include information in request headers. Request headers are information or metadata about the current request. They are most often entered by the Web browser, but can also be added by Web proxy servers. Some examples of information contained in request headers are the name and version of the client, the MIME types the browser supports, and the user's preferred language. See Table 6–1 for a description of some common request headers.

TABLE 6–1 Common Request Headers

`Accept`	These are the MIME types accepted by the requesting browser. Optionally, they can have a quality factor included.
`Accept-Language`	Here, a browser may indicate which languages it prefers. ISO country codes are used to accomplish this. Some examples are `"en"` for English or `"de"` for German. More than one language can be specified, delimited by commas. Optionally, they can have a quality factor included.
`Cookie`	If a browser finds a cookie in its cookie file matching the domain of this server, it will send it along with every request.
`Host`	This is the name of the server to which the request was sent. The request line only specifies part of the URL, which does not include the server. The Web server can use this information to see which hostname is explicitly desired and serve the right page. This removes the necessity of having different IP addresses for virtual servers.
`Referer`	This is the URL of the page on which this server was referred. This is traditionally spelled incorrectly.
`User-Agent`	This is a browser's ID. It describes the software used as well as the version. Optionally, it includes the default ISO country code.

In the same way parameters can be accessed in "raw" format, the values of HTTP headers can be retrieved "as-is". There are also a number of convenience methods for retrieving certain headers and data types.

The basic "raw" method is `getHeader()`. This method takes a `String` argument that describes the header name field. It returns a `String` that contains the value of the requested header, or `null` if the header does not exist. Very similar to `getHeader()` are `getIntHeader()` and `getDateHeader()`. Both `getIntHeader()` and `getDateHeader()` take the same `String` header name argument as does `getHeader()`, but they return an `int` and a `date` object, respectively.

Retrieving request header information faces many of the same challenges as getting parameter information, as they both are stored in name/value pairs. For example, what if the names of the headers are unknown? Similar to `getParameterNames()`, there is `getHeaderNames()`, which will return an `Enumeration` of the request header field names.

In addition to these four methods, the Java Servlet 2.2 specification adds three new methods for gathering header information. The Java Servlet 2.2 API is utilized by the JSP 1.1 specification, so any JSP 1.1 or above-compliant engine can recognize these methods. The first method again builds on experience from the parameter methods. While it is rare, multiple headers with the same name bearing different values are possible. In this situation, `getHeaders()` can be utilized. `getHeaders()` has a `String` that describes a header field name as an argument. It returns an `Enumeration` of the different values for the specified header.

Additionally, the Java Servlet 2.2 API specification adds the `getLocale()` and `getLocales()` methods. These methods are actually inherited from the `ServletRequest` object from which the `HttpServletRequest` object is derived. These methods receive their information from the `Accept-Language` header. `getLocale()` returns a string that describes the ISO country code of the preferred language. Since more than one value can be specified, the `getLocales()` method is also provided. The `getLocales()` method returns an `Enumeration` of the specified language country codes in order of decreasing preference.

The information stored in headers gives some very specific information about a Web client to the JSP author, and allows for very specific content to be sent to the user. One area where this is especially useful is in internationalization. As the Web is growing by leaps and bounds, there is a need to expand large sites to multiple languages. Further, if a page can be tailored to the user's language of preference without the user having to specify one, it makes the Web page much more user-friendly. Fortunately, 4.0 and above browsers specify which language is preferred in the `Accept-Language` header.

Take a look at Script 6.2 to see a page that tailors "Hello World" to a user's preferred language.

Script 6.2
HelloWorld.jsp

```
<!DOCTYPE HTML PUBLIC "-//W3C//DTD HTML 4.0 Final//EN">
```

```
<%@ page contentType="text/html; charset=UTF-8" %>
<%@ page import="java.util.*" %>
<HTML><HEAD><TITLE>Stitch Magazine!</TITLE></HEAD>
<BODY BGCOLOR="white">

<%!
  Hashtable helloHash = new Hashtable();

  public void jspInit() {
    helloHash.put("en", "Hello World");
    helloHash.put("fr", "Bonjour Monde");
    helloHash.put("de", "Hallo Welt");
    helloHash.put("it", "Ciao Mondo");
    helloHash.put("pt", "Hello Mundo");
    helloHash.put("es", "Hola Mundo");
    helloHash.put("ja",
        "\u4eca\u65e5\u306f\u4e16\u754c");
    helloHash.put("zh", "\u4F60\u597D\u4E16\u754C");
    helloHash.put("ko",
        "\uC548\uB155\uD558\uC138\uC694\uC138\uACC4");
    helloHash.put("ru",
        "\u0417\u0434\u0440\u0430\u0432\u0441\u0442"
        + "\u0432\u0443\u0439, \u041C\u0438\u0440");
  }

  public String getGreeting (String Languages) {
    String lang = new String();
    StringTokenizer langPrefs =
        new StringTokenizer(Languages, ",");

    while ((!helloHash.containsKey(lang)) &&
           (langPrefs.hasMoreTokens())) {
      lang = langPrefs.nextToken().substring(0,2);
    }

    if ((!helloHash.containsKey(lang)) ||
        (lang == null)) {
      lang = "en";
    }

    return (String)helloHash.get(lang);
  }

%>

<%
  String Languages
      = request.getHeader("Accept-Language");
%>
<H2>
<%= getGreeting(Languages) %><BR>
```

```
    </BODY>
</HTML>
```

With Japanese selected as the language of choice, the output of HelloWorld.jsp should look something like Figure 6–3.

There is really no magic here. HelloWorld.jsp uses Unicode to display its characters, using the UTF-8 character set. Described simply, Unicode contains all of the characters in the alphabets of several hundred languages. Since the UTF-8 version of Unicode is used here, strings in the standard ASCII range can be added simply by specifying a string. Characters for other languages have to be specified with escape sequences. Unicode character escapes are signified by the string "\u", followed by a hexadecimal string of four digits containing the number of the specific character desired. Unicode escapes can be used to display almost every character in the world's common written languages.

Another important thing to point out is that the client must have a font installed that will display the characters needed. There are many font sets available on the Internet that display fonts of a specific language, and even a few which try to cover the range of Unicode. The client must have its browser's preferences set to map Unicode or UTF-8 character sets to the correct font. Additionally, the client must have language preferences set up in its browser.

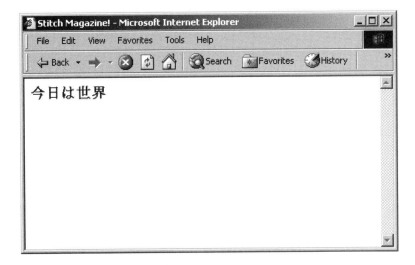

FIGURE 6–3 Output of HelloWorld.jsp

Take a look at the `jspInit()` function of `HelloWorld.jsp`:

```
helloHash.put("en", "Hello World");
helloHash.put("fr", "Bonjour Monde");
helloHash.put("de", "Hallo Welt");
helloHash.put("it", "Ciao Mondo");
helloHash.put("pt", "Hello Mundo");
helloHash.put("es", "Hola Mundo");
helloHash.put("ja",
    "\u4eca\u65e5\u306f\u4e16\u754c");
helloHash.put("zh", "\u4F60\u597D\u4E16\u754C");
helloHash.put("ko",
    "\uC548\uB155\uD558\uC138\uC694\uC138\uACC4");
helloHash.put("ru",
    "\u0417\u0434\u0440\u0430\u0432\u0441\u0442"
  + "\u0432\u0443\u0439, \u041C\u0438\u0440");
```

Here, the ISO country code is entered as a key into a `hash table` called `helloHash`. The corresponding string "`Hello World`" is entered as a value, described in the characters of the specified language. There is no translation done here. The JSP author had to know how to write "Hello World" in the specific characters of each language.

Next, skip down to the bottom of `HelloWorld.jsp` to see the two lines that get the header and call the workhorse function:

```
<%
    String Languages
        = request.getHeader("Accept-Language");
%>
<H2>
<%= getGreeting(Languages) %><BR>
```

The first line of code simply gets the text value associated with the header `Accept-Language`. Remember that this is a comma-delimited `string` listing the preferred language of the user in order of preference. For example, the string might be "`en,ru,ja`", which would mean that the author prefers English, Russian, or Japanese, in that order. Note that in a JSP 1.1 or above-compliant engine, the `getLocales()` function could be used here to gather the country code information.

Next, the JSP expression calls the workhorse function `getGreeting()`, sending the header value as an argument. This function returns the proper `string` for the specified language to the output stream. Now take a look at `getGreeting()`, which does the real work:

```
public String getGreeting (String Languages) {
  String lang = new String();
  StringTokenizer langPrefs
    = new StringTokenizer(Languages, ",");

  while ((!helloHash.containsKey(lang)) &&
        (langPrefs.hasMoreTokens())) {
    lang = langPrefs.nextToken().substring(0,2);
  }

  if ((!helloHash.containsKey(lang)) ||
      (lang == null)) {
    lang = "en";
  }

  return (String)helloHash.get(lang);
}
```

There are two strings defined: Language, which is sent from the caller, and lang, which serves as a placeholder for the current section of the Language string that is being matched. To break Language up into the different languages it specifies, a StringTokenizer is used, with a comma used to separate each section of data. Using the above example of "en,ru,ja" as the Language string, lang would be set to "en", "ru", and "ja" alternatively each time through the while loop.

Why are only the first two letters of the country code taken? Sometimes, more information is given for each country. For example, instead of "zh" for Chinese, "zh-TW" might be specified for the Taiwanese dialect of Chinese. The Web browser might also append a numeric weight to each language specified. As the helloHash Hashtable is built around only the country code itself, the rest of the information is discarded.

The while loop checks to see if the preferred language has a match in the helloHash hash table by using the method containsKey(). If the first language has no match, it goes on to each other language specified. If there is a match, the while loop is broken with lang still set to the language that had a match. In this way, each language specified by the user is checked for a match until one is found that is supported by the JSP page. If no match is found, or if there was no language specified (where lang == null), the last if statement will set lang to "en" for English, which was chosen as the default language. The final line returns the helloHash value for lang.

The HelloWorld.jsp example makes it obvious that there is a lot of information that can be derived from headers to create very specific responses for a client.

6.3.1 Cookies

Method Signature:

```
Cookie[] request.getCookie()
```

No discussion of request header information would be complete without mentioning getting cookies. A cookie is a system by which a server can store information on a client's machine. A server sets a cookie by sending it in a response header. Each cookie has a specific time length before it will "expire" and be removed from the client machine. By default, this is when the current Web client application is closed.

When a cookie is set, it is matched to a specific URL. When the client requests a URL, the Web browser checks to see if it has a cookie in its cookie file that matches the URL. If there is a match, the cookie is included in the request header. To store cookies, the Java Servlet API, on which the Java JSP API is built, creates a Cookie object.

While cookie information can be received as a String by using the method getHeader("cookie"), managing multiple cookies and translating them into Cookie objects is a surmountable task. Luckily, the getCookie() method is provided to do just that. The getCookie() method takes no argument and returns an array of Cookie objects. If there were no cookies specified, it would return null.

6.3.2 Attributes

Method Signature:

```
String request.getAttribute(String)
```

Method Signature:

```
Enumeration request.getAttributeNames()
```

Besides parameters and headers there is a third type of information that can be derived from the request object: attributes. Attributes are JSP engine-specific and contain information about the request object itself, or request metadata. To get attribute information, the request object provides the getAttribute() method. One common attribute is the SSL certificate used by the client to make an encrypted session. For example:

```
<%=
request.getAttribute("javax.servlet.request.X509Certificate")
%>
```

This will only work if the JSP engine supports this attribute and the actual connection made by a client was done using SSL. Similar to parameters and headers, attributes have a `getAttributeNames()` function. This function takes no argument and returns an `Enumeration` object listing the attributes for the current request object. The only way to find out all of the request attributes supported a given JSP engine is to read the JSE engine's specific documentation.

6.3.3 Server Information

Method Signature:

```
String application.getServerInfo()
```

Method Signature:

```
String application.getRealPath(String)
```

In addition to the `request` object, information about the specific configuration of the JSP engine can be accessed through the implicit `application` object. Remember that the `application` object is an instance of `javax.servlet.ServletContext`. This means it has specific information about the JSP engine as well as the operating system as it relates to the server.

One piece of information made available to the application object is the JSP engine name and version number. This data also may contain other information such as the JRE version or operating system. This string can be obtained by using the `getServerInfo()` method. It takes no arguments and returns a `String`. For example:

```
<%= application.getServerInfo() %>
```

will return a string similar to:

```
JavaServer Web Dev Kit/1.0 EA (JSP 1.0; Servlet 2.1; Java 1.2.2;
Windows NT 5.0 x86; java.vendor=Sun Microsystems Inc.)
```

This string was returned by the JSWDK on a Windows 2000 box.

Another method of the `ServletContext` object is `getRealPath()`. The `getRealPath()` method takes a `String` that describes part of a URL. The method returns a `String` that contains the full path of the file that matches the URL. For example:

```
<%= application.getRealPath(request.getRequestURI()) %>
```

This takes the URL of the current page and returns the path of the file on the local file system. In this case, it returns: `D:\jswdk1.0\javadesktop\test.jsp`.

◆ 6.4 Recap

Overall, the JSP API specification provides several different methods for accessing information about a client's request and the local server environment. It is important to remember that this is the only information that a JSP program can use to define specific content. In the next chapter, the response object will be covered in detail. In Chapter 8, "Tracking Sessions," sessions, which help tie specific sets of request/response pairs to an individual client, will be discussed.

chapter

7 Sending Information

IN THIS CHAPTER

- Using the `response` Object
- Setting Cookies
- Handling Errors
- Recap

JSP can perform a lot of complex tasks on the server ranging from manag-ing a database to performing complex math. However, it's important to keep in mind that JSP is primarily designed to describe data being sent back to the user.

Examples in previous chapters have shown how easy it is to send simple information from a JSP page. Using the HTML or XML template, the methods of the `out` *object, or the expression tags (*`<%=...%>`*), the JSP author can generate content for the resulting page. The process of send-ing simple data really does not involve much more than that.*

Unfortunately, real-world data is often not quite so simple that it will easily fall into the default categories. In many cases, the JSP author will need to be able to take control of the output and give the server explicit instructions on how the response should be constructed.

◆ 7.1 Using the `response` Object

A client requests a page by building an HTTP request and the results are sent back in an HTTP response. The HTTP response can contain the data returned from the request or an error indicating that the request was not successful. Typically, a successful request will include the data and information describing the data in the HTTP response.

Normally, the HTTP response is managed entirely by the server. All information passed through the server gets put into the standard group; the response is built, and then sent back to the client.

To send data that is not managed entirely by the server requires manipulating the HTTP response. Carefully controlling the HTTP response is the most important aspect of sending complex information. JSP provides an interface into manipulating the response through the `HttpServletResponse` object, which is exposed to the JSP author through the implicit `response` object.

In Chapter 1, "An Overview of JSP," the HTTP response was shown to be composed of three basic parts: the status, headers, and data. To send more complex information, a more detailed understanding of these three components is required.

7.1.1 The HTTP Status

The HTTP status is set to indicate the actual status of the request. Typically, this will contain "`succeeded`", "`failed`", or some other condition information that directs the client how to respond. In essence, the HTTP status line defines how the rest of the response will be received.

A typical HTTP status line is shown here:

```
HTTP/1.1 200 OK
```

The HTTP status begins by stating the protocol it is going to use. Since this is an HTTP status, the protocol information typically reflects the specific version of the HTTP protocol to follow, 1.0 or 1.1.

Following that is an integer value that represents the actual results of the request. This may also be followed by a human-readable value corresponding to the integer result.

Table 7–1 shows some of the more common HTTP status codes. This table shows the status code, followed by its Java servlet constant, and a description of the status. The "`404 Not`

Found" and "500 Internal Server Error" status codes may look very familiar to some people; other status codes are only used behind-the-scenes.

TABLE 7–1 Common HTTP Status Codes

200 OK	SC_OK

This status is sent when a request was processed completely and without errors.

204 No Content	SC_NO_CONTENT

Indicates that the request was processed, but there is no data to return.

301 Moved Permanently	SC_MOVED_PERMANTENTLY

This indicates that the URI has been changed permanently. Most clients will look in the header information for a new location.

302 Moved Temporarily	SC_MOVED_TEMPORARILY

The URI is temporarily relocated. Most clients will look in the header information for a new location.

401 Unauthorized	SC_UNAUTHORIZED

Authentication was not successful and access is being denied.

403 Forbidden	SC_FORBIDDEN

This indicates that the page is restricted and the client is not allowed access.

404 Not Found	SC_NOT_FOUND

The requested document does not exist.

500 Internal Server Error	SC_INTERNAL_SERVER_ERROR

Errors on the server prevent the request from being completed.

503 Service Unavailable	SC_SERVICE_UNAVAILABLE

The server is temporarily overloaded and unable to complete the request.

The response object provides the sendError() and setStatus() methods, allowing the JSP author to set the HTTP status code that is sent back to the user. Both of these methods behave in a similar fashion. Some extra logic separates sendError() as the method to send status codes that indicate a failed request. The setStatus() method should be used to set all other HTTP status codes.

These methods typically accept an integer value or constant as the argument, which will correspond directly to the value sent. Some of these methods also allow an error to include a text message.

```
void response.sendError(int sc)
void response.sendError(int sc, String msg)
void response.setStatus(int sc)
void response.setStatus(int sc, String msg)
```

Also note that errors are really the only form of HTTP status that may need an expanded message, so `void response.send-Status(int sc, String msg)` has been deprecated because it was ambiguous.

7.1.2 HTTP Headers

Immediately following the HTTP status line are the HTTP headers. These are a series of name/value pairs that contain information about the server and the document being returned. The HTTP headers section can be any length and a single blank line marks its end.

A typical set of HTTP headers is displayed here:

```
Date: Sun, 08 Dec 1999 18:16:31 GMT
Server: Apache/1.3.9 (Unix) ApacheJServ/1.0
Last-Modified: Tue, 22 Jun 1999 05:12:38 GMT
ETag: "d828b-371-376f1b46"
Accept-Ranges: bytes
Connection: close
Content-Type: text/html
```

The most important thing to note about these HTTP headers is that this is information the server specifically wants the client to have. They may not trigger a response on the client side, but they are intended to direct the behavior of the client. This may include time stamps for client-side caching, the type of data that will be sent, or information to identify the server.

While there is no complete list of HTTP headers that can be used, there are some very common headers. Table 7–2 shows some of the more common HTTP headers used by many Web pages.

TABLE 7–2 Common HTTP Headers

`Content-type`	This is the MIME type of the data being sent in the HTTP response body.

`Connection`	This indicates whether the server will maintain a constantly open connection. If the server will support this, the value is set to `keep-alive`; otherwise, the value is close.
`Location`	This header is only read by the client when the server sets the status to `301 Moved Permanently` or `302 Moved Temporarily`. This specifies a URI that should be used for a new location. Most browsers will automatically follow this link when the status is set appropriately.
`Expires`	This date field specifies when the document should become invalid for caching purposes.
`Cache-Control`	(HTTP1.1 only) This allows control over specific caching issues that relate to this document. Common values are `no-cache`, `no-store` (`no-store` indicates that the client, caching proxies, and squid engines should never cache the document), and `maxage=n` (to expire the document in n seconds).
`Pragma`	(HTTP1.0—replaced by `Cache-Control` in HTTP1.1) `Pragma` allows extremely limited control on the cache. The only valid value is `no-cache`, which instructs the browser to never cache this document.

The `response` object provides the JSP author with several methods that can be used to manipulate the response headers.

```
void response.addHeader(String name, String value)
void resp onse.setHeader(String name, String value)
void response.addIntHeader(String name, int value)
void response.setIntHeader(String name, int value)
void response.addDateHeader(String name, long date)
void response.setDateHeader(String name, long date)
```

The primary difference between these methods is the type of data that each sets in the response header. The type of data accepted by each method is fairly self-explanatory by the method signature.

Understanding the difference between `add` and `set` methods is less obvious. The difference really involves the fact that HTTP headers can have more than one entry with the same named key. The `add` methods will create a new name/value pair that may be in addition to an existing pair with that same name. The `set` methods will overwrite the previous pairs that have the same named key.

These methods allow the JSP author to modify or create an HTTP header. However, there are a series of convenience methods that modify the most often used headers.

`Content-type` is a very important header that defines the MIME type of the document being sent. The following method has been made to allow easier access to changing the MIME type of the document:

```
void response.setContentType(String type)
```

ESSENTIAL NOTE: `CONTENT-TYPE`

`Content-type` is almost always included to define the MIME type of the data carried in the response body. By default, the server, based on what the server knows of the data, sets `Content-type`.

Changing the `Content-type` header can dramatically change the response on the client. For example, a `Content-type` of `text/html` will be interpreted as HTML; however, setting it to `image/png` will force the browser to interpret the data as a `.png` graphic file. The Unicode example in the previous chapter used the `Content-type` to define the data as `UTF-8` data as opposed to standard `html/text`.

Of course, many of these methods would not be useful unless the JSP author could check the header for a specific named key. This is exactly what the `containsHeader()` method is for.

```
boolean response.containsHeader(String name)
```

The `containsHeader` method simple returns `true` if the named key exists, allowing the JSP author a means to check before overwriting.

7.1.3 Other Methods of the response Object

The `response` object also has some methods, which do not deal with just the HTTP status or HTTP headers. Some of these methods involve merging the status and header information, and others are convenience methods that have no direct relation to the HTTP response.

Redirecting a client to an alternate URI is a relatively common occurrence. This could be done by first setting the status to `SC_MOVED_TEMPORARILY`, and then setting the location header to the destination URI. For example:

```
response.setStatus(SC_MOVED_TEMPORARILY);
response.setHeader ("Location",
"http://localhost:8080/");
```

These two method calls are so interdependent that they have been converted into a single method:

```
void response.sendRedirect ("http://localhost:8080/");
```

Script 7.1 shows a simple JSP page that does "round-robin" load balancing. "Round-robin" load balancing is a way to distribute requests across multiple servers; it's not very sophisticated, but it works in many situations.

The "round robin" is accomplished by using the sendRedirect method of the response object. The actual list of servers is implemented using a circular queue stored in a vector.

Some people may notice that some HTML information was included in the bottom of the JSP page. This is done because some browsers process the page enough to make the screen "blink" before forwarding. The small amount of HTML sets the background color to the color of the new page, which makes the "blink" significantly less noticeable.

Script 7.1
roundRobin.jsp

```
<!DOCTYPE HTML PUBLIC "-//W3C//DTD HTML 4.0 Final//EN">

<%@ page import ="java.util.Vector"%>

<%!
  Vector servers = new Vector();

  public void jspInit() {
    servers.addElement("http://server1.javadesktop.com/");
    servers.addElement("http://server2.javadesktop.com/");
    servers.addElement("http://server3.javadesktop.com/");
  }

  synchronized public String nextInQueue (Vector queue) {
    // implement a cyclic queue
    String item = (String)queue.firstElement();
    queue.removeElementAt(0);
    queue.addElement (item);
    return (item);
  }
%>
```

```
<%
    response.sendRedirect(nextInQueue(servers));
%>

<HTML>
<BODY BGCOLOR="#ffffff">
</BODY>
</HTML>
```

◆ 7.2 Setting Cookies

Quite often, a server will send cookies to a client to store little bits of information. This information is managed by the client and may be requested by the server at a later time.

Information on retrieving cookies was discussed in the previous chapter. Setting cookies is a little more complicated because it involves first creating the cookie, then sending it to the client.

ESSENTIAL NOTE: COOKIES

A lot of people know what cookies are; many Web developers know how to use them, but most people don't really know how they work.

In reality, cookies are really just a special kind of HTTP header. This special header contains a comma-separated list of values that describes a name/value pair, an expiration date, and some control information.

Unlike a standard HTTP response header, the information sent in a cookie is saved on the client. The client will then send information back to the server if it matches the URI and hostname specified in the cookie.

Since the client manages the cookie, the client can impose additional restrictions about how cookies are accepted. It is also the responsibility of the client to expire old cookies.

7.2.1 Building a Cookie

JSP represents cookies with a `Cookie` object. This object is created with the following constructor:

```
public Cookie (String name, String Value)
```

A cookie is normally composed of several attributes. The most important data is the name/value pair, which is the data the server would retrieve from the cookie. But the cookie also contains information on when to expire the cookie and when to give out the cookie.

The name/value pair that is stored in the cookie is established when the cookie is first instantiated using `new Cookie (String name, String Value)`. Other attributes default to standard values determined by the server, but they can be changed using methods of the `Cookie` object.

```
void Cookie.setMaxAge (int expire)
```

By using the `setMaxAge` method, the JSP author can set the lifespan of a cookie. By default, the maximum age is set to a negative value. This makes the cookie "temporary"; the cookie will be destroyed when the browser exits.

Cookies can also be made pseudo-permanent by setting a positive integer value. A cookie has a lifespan that is measured in seconds since it was received. These kinds of cookies are discarded by the client when they get too old.

Cookies can also be destroyed by setting the `setMaxAge` method. By setting the value to zero (0), the browser will destroy the cookie immediately.

```
void Cookie.setDomain (String pattern)
```

This method restricts accessing cookies based on the name of the server. The default is set to match only the server that sent the cookie. This prevents any other server from retrieving a cookie set by that server.

`setDomain` can be set to match specific domain name pattern. Domain patterns can allow a set of servers under a similar subdomain to have access to the same cookie. Domain name patterns always begin with a dot and will only allow access to hosts (not subdomains) that match this pattern. For example, by setting a domain pattern of `'.javadesktop.com'`, a cookie could be received by `'www.javadesktop.com'` and `'www2.javadesktop.com'`.

```
void Cookie.setPath (String uri)
```

A specific path on the server can also restrict the cookie by using the `setPath` method. Applications at the same directory level or under the specified URI are also able to access the cookie. For example, if `setPath` was set to `/JSP/catalog`, then `/JSP/catalog/list.jsp` and `/JSP/catalog/admin/addNewItem.jsp` would be able to access the same cookies.

```
void Cookie.setSecure (boolean flag)
```

The setSecure method will require a cookie to be sent only via a secure channel, such as an SSL connection. By default, cookies do not have this restriction.

7.2.2 Sending a Cookie

When a cookie is created and configured properly, it still needs to be send out to the client. This is done using the addCookie() method provided by the response object.

```
void response.addCookie(Cookie cookie)
```

This method will add the cookie to the response headers. When the page is sent, the cookie will be retrieved and stored by the server. The next request sent by the client should contain the cookie information.

7.2.3 Using Cookies

Script 7.2 shows an example of getting and setting cookies. This is a fairly complex example that stores the name of the user.

Script 7.2
userGreeting.jsp

```
<!DOCTYPE HTML PUBLIC "-//W3C//DTD HTML 4.0 Final//EN">

<%@ page import ="java.util.*"%>

<%!
  Hashtable cookieTable (Cookie[] cookies) {
    Hashtable cookieTable = new Hashtable();

    if (cookies != null) {
      for (int i=0; i < cookies.length; i++) {
        cookieTable.put(cookies[i].getName(),cookies[i].getValue());
      }
    }

    return cookieTable;
  }
%>

<%
  Cookie myCookie;
```

```
String username = new String();
Hashtable cookies = cookieTable(request.getCookies());
String newLogin = request.getParameter("name");

if (cookies.containsKey("name")) {
  username = (String)cookies.get("name");
}

if (newLogin != null) {
  if (newLogin.equals("")) {
    myCookie = new Cookie("name", "");
    myCookie.setMaxAge(0);
    username = null;
  } else {
    myCookie = new Cookie("name", newLogin);
    myCookie.setMaxAge(3600);
    username = newLogin;
  }

  /*
     It is important to change the domain to
     your domain name in order for this to work
  */
  myCookie.setDomain(".javadesktop.com");

  response.addCookie(myCookie);
}
%>

<HTML><HEAD><TITLE>Stitch Magazine!</TITLE></HEAD>

<STYLE>
.login {
  position: relative; border: 1px; margin: 1px;
  background-color:#bbbbbb; text-align: right;
  font-family: Arial,Helvetica,sans-serif;
  font-size: 9pt; color:#000000;
}
</STYLE>

<BODY BGCOLOR="#ffffff">

<DIV CLASS="login">
<% if (username == null || username.equals("")) { %>

You look like a new user!<BR>
<FORM METHOD="get" ACTION="<%= request.getRequestURI() %>">
Create a login by entering your name:<BR>
<INPUT TYPE="text" SIZE="8" NAME="name">
<INPUT TYPE="submit" VALUE="login">
</FORM>
```

```
<% } else { %>

Welcome back, <%= username %><BR>
<%= new java.util.Date() %>
<FORM METHOD="get" ACTION="<%= request.getRequestURI() %>">
<INPUT TYPE="hidden" NAME="name" VALUE="">
<INPUT TYPE="submit" VALUE="logout">
</FORM>

<% } %>

</DIV>
</BODY>
</HTML>
```

When run for the first time, Script 7.2 should look similar to Figure 7–1.

In this example, the cookies are retrieved and read into a `Hashtable` by the `cookieTable` method. Using a `Hashtable` to store the cookies allows for rapid searching to find a particular cookie.

The majority of the work involved in managing the cookies happens here:

```
if (cookies.containsKey("name")) {
  username = (String)cookies.get("name");
}

if (newLogin != null) {
```

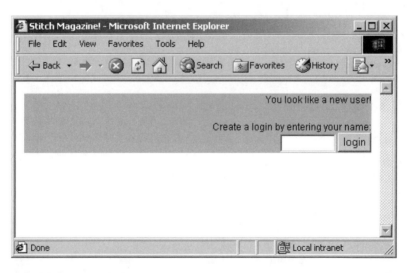

FIGURE 7–1 userGreeting.jsp

```
if (newLogin.equals("")) {
  Cookie newCookie = new Cookie("name", "");
  newCookie.setMaxAge(0);
  username = null;
} else {
  Cookie newCookie = new Cookie("name", newLogin);
  username = newLogin;
}
newCookie.setDomain(".javadesktop.com");
response.addCookie(newCookie);
}
```

Take particular notice of the functions that were used to manage the cookie. The name/value pair is set at the time of creating the cookie. The cookie is not actually sent to the client until `response.addCookie(newCookie)` is called.

Deleting the cookie is accomplished by changing the value of `setMaxAge` to zero. This instructs the client to expire the cookie immediately.

Also note that `Cookie.setDomain(".javadesktop.com")` sets the domain to match any host on the `javadesktop.com` domain. This prevents multiple Web servers from having to manage separate cookies; all hosts on the domain share the same cookie.

◆ 7.3 Handling Errors

Things should never go wrong. JSP pages released into production should be tested, debugged, and released as enterprise applications.

Of course, in the real world, things do go wrong even with applications that have undergone the most rigorous testing and debugging. Many of these errors can be caught and handled using Java's built-in exception handling. In addition, JSP provides some great resources to help the JSP author manage error conditions.

Sending the fully detailed and ugly error details to the client is not particularly useful. So, JSP pages should also always specify the `errorPage` page directive attribute. This allows the JSP author to deal with any uncaught exceptions and present a nice-looking front-end page to the client.

Using `errorPage` will also allow the JSP author to build additional functions that should run to help deal with errors appropriately. They might include functions to log the error on the server using the `application.log()` method. It is even possible to forward the resulting problem to another location based on the specific form of problem that occurred.

Below are two examples. Script 7.3 shows a page that is really not very practical; it is designed to simply throw an error and nothing else. What is interesting is the effect of the `errorPage` shown in Script 7.4.

Script 7.3
errorGen.jsp

```
<%@ page errorPage = "errorPage.jsp" %>
<%
  if (true) {
    throw new Exception ("Just testing");
  }
%>
```

Script 7.4 sets the `isErrorPage` page directive attribute so that it will be recognized as an error page.

Script 7.4
errorPage.jsp

```
<!DOCTYPE HTML PUBLIC "-//W3C//DTD HTML 4.0 Final//EN">
<%@ page isErrorPage="true" %>
<%@ page import="java.io.*" %>

<%!
 String showError (HttpServletRequest req, Throwable ex)
      throws IOException {
    StringBuffer err = new StringBuffer();

    err.append("Uncaught runtime error --\n");
    err.append("        URI: ");
    err.append(req.getRequestURI()).append("\n");
    err.append("Extra Path: ");
    err.append(req.getPathInfo()).append("\n");

    ByteArrayOutputStream baos
      = new ByteArrayOutputStream();
    PrintWriter pw = new PrintWriter (baos, true);
    ex.printStackTrace (pw);

    err.append("      Stack: ");
    err.append(baos.toString()).append("\n");

    baos.close();

    return (err.toString());
  }
%>
```

```
<%
 response.setStatus (response.SC_INTERNAL_SERVER_ERROR);
%>
<HTML><HEAD><TITLE>Stitch Magazine!</TITLE></HEAD>
<STYLE>
body {
  background-color: #ffffff; color: #000000;
}
.error {
  position: absolute; top: 50px;
  font-family: courier, monospaced; font-size: 11pt;
  font-weight: bold;
}
</STYLE>
<BODY>
<%
  String error = showError(request, exception);
  application.log (error);
%>
<DIV CLASS="error">
500 -- Internal Server Error<BR>
Error in: <%= request.getRequestURI() %><BR>
Reason: <%= exception.getMessage() %><BR>
</DIV>
</BODY>
</HTML>
```

When Script 7.3 is viewed, it should display Script 7.4 (see Figure 7–2).

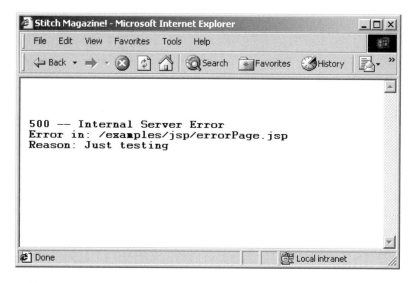

FIGURE 7–2 errorGen.jsp

Notice that the `request` object used in this example appears the same as the `request` object from the original page. In fact, even the `getRequestURI()` method returns the URI of the original page and not the error page. The client will also not see a change; however, the browser will still show the originally requested page in the `Location:` line. Because of this, it is possible to direct the error in such a way that the client may never know an error occurred at all.

Also take note of the `exception` object, which contains the exception thrown by the original URI. In this example, the information is just logged, but this could also be used to react more appropriately based on the type of error that occurred.

Lastly, one of the more interesting features of this example is the use of the `application` object. The data is actually being recorded directly to the server's logs by using the `log` method of the `application` object.

```
application.log (error)
```

◆ 7.4 Recap

There are many powerful features in JSP that allow specific client responses. Understanding different HTTP headers and response codes, as well as how to access them with methods of the `response` object, gives the JSP author a low-level ability to manipulate what the user can see. Complex tasks such as manipulating cookies and creating custom error pages are made easy with convenience methods. The next chapter, "Tracking Sessions," will cover how to tie specific request/response pairs to individual clients.

8 Tracking Sessions

JSP is typically used to create HTML or XML pages that are delivered using HTTP. Previous chapters have discussed HTTP requests and responses. One of the limitations of HTTP is that it is a stateless and connectionless protocol. This means that the protocol has no recollection of any transaction that occurred in the past. Each new request from the client creates a whole new transaction that has no relation to any past, concurrent, or future transaction. The client makes a request, the server completes the request to the best of its abilities, and then the transaction is completed and finished.

Without state, each request must contain everything that the server might need to complete the request. In a basic sense, this means that even something as simple as displaying the user's name on a page means that the requestor needs to send that information in each request.

Unfortunately, this model does not fulfill the requirements of modern applications. It would be like a dialog between two people where whenever one person talked, both would forget everything that was said previously.

◆ 8.1 Tracking Data between Requests

Needless to say, most applications in use today need to keep at least some constant information about previous transactions. Knowing whether a user has already logged in, keeping a list of items in a shopping cart, or simply knowing that the user wants to have a blue background all require some memory of previous requests. So of course, many ingenious strategies have been developed to work around these limitations.

8.1.1 Hidden Form Fields

A relatively simple way to track data between user requests is to use an HTML form. Hidden form fields are simple and effective for maintaining small amounts of data between a few forms.

To use hidden form fields, the server takes the request data and puts it back into a form on the next page. The server must do this each time or all the data is lost. This method puts the majority of the burden back on the client. In essence, the client is told to remember all the previous information and send it the next time. Again to use the analogy of a dialog between two people, it would be as if the entire previous conversation had to be repeated before a new idea could be added.

Hidden form fields are one of the oldest methods of preserving state information that are still in use today. The fact that it is still in use seems to indicate that it fills an important need, in particular where a task is not complex, but still needs to keep some "state" information. A common case where this might used would be where a user must fill in a form that is mailed to a Webmaster. If the user forgets an important field, it can be specifically requested on the next "page;" all of the previous data is stored on the same page unbeknownst to the user.

It is important to note that this method will only work to and from HTML forms. Changes to state information outside of a form cannot be easily done using hidden form fields.

8.1.2 A Brief Tutorial on JavaMail

The following example sends an email to a user based on the fields put into a form. In this example, email is handled using a Java package called JavaMail. The JavaMail API should already be installed on systems where the Java 2 Enterprise Edition was installed, and can be added to any Java 2 installation. The Java-Mail API also requires the JavaBeans Activation Framework

(JAF), which is also installed with Java 2 Enterprise Edition, or can be installed separately.

The JavaMail API creates an abstraction from the actual mail system, providing a platform-independent and protocol-independent framework to access mail. The system works by providing a basic framework with service providers to implement particular protocols. JavaMail provides just about every service that an email client or even an email server might need.

In this particular example, the requirements are very small. An email needs to be created and sent to a single user. Creating the email in the example is basically separated into three steps; compose the text of the message, set up the server information, and send the email.

The creation of the email message is simple. The actual body of the email just needs to wind up in a `String`. Later, when the message is sent, it will include this `String`.

Setting up the server information is fairly straightforward. First, data from the system is received and anything that might need to change is overridden or added. In this case, `mail.smtp.host` is set to the mail delivery host. To set the server properties, these two lines are used:

```
Properties props = System.getProperties();
props.put("mail.smtp.host", mailhost);
Session emailsession = Session.getDefaultInstance(props, null);
```

It is important to note that the string "`mail.smtp.host`" must be replaced with a valid Internet SMTP server URL for this code to work.

Finally, the mail is created and sent. This requires filling out the header fields needed to make a valid email, then calling the `Transport.send()` method from JavaMail. The following list of commands is what actually builds and sends the email:

```
Message email = new MimeMessage(emailsession);
email.setFrom(new InternetAddress(req.getServletPath()));
InternetAddress[] address = {
                new InternetAddress(formRecipient) };
email.setRecipients(Message.RecipientType.TO,address);
email.setSubject(req.getServletPath());
email.setSentDate(new Date());
email.setHeader("X-Mailer","MailFormJava");
email.setText(message);
Transport.send(email);
```

8.1.3 A Mail Form Example

Script 8.1 shows an example of a very simple form that uses hidden fields to store data between pages. Once all the required fields have been filled, JavaMail is then used to send the email to the user.

The examples in this chapter are set up slightly differently than previous examples in that they use <jsp:include> to add new components to the page. This effectively means that each example will include multiple sets of code, where one of the sets will represent a "wrapper." Script 8.2 is the wrapper for Script 8.1; it generates the proper header and footer to make the page behave properly on a browser.

Script 8.1
mailForm.jsp

```
<%@ page import =
    "javax.mail.*,javax.mail.internet.*,
    javax.activation.*,java.util.*"
%>

<%!
  private final String formRecipient = "webmaster@javadesktop.com";
  private final String mailhost = "mail.javadesktop.com";
  private final String senderAddress = "mail form@javadesktop.com";

  class formField {
    String name;
    boolean required;

    formField (String name, boolean required) {
      this.name = name;
      this.required = required;
    }
  }

  Vector fieldList = new Vector();

  public void jspInit() {
    fieldList.add(new formField("Name", true));
    fieldList.add(new formField("Address", false));
    fieldList.add(new formField("City", false));
    fieldList.add(new formField("State", false));
    fieldList.add(new formField("ZIP Code", false));
    fieldList.add(new formField("Day Phone", false));
    fieldList.add(new formField("Evening Phone", false));
    fieldList.add(new formField("Email", true));
```

```
      fieldList.add(new formField("Website", false));
}

String displayField (String name) {
  StringBuffer formOut = new StringBuffer();

  formOut.append("<input type=\"text\" name=\"")
          .append(name)
          .append("\">\n");

  return (formOut.toString());
}

String storeField (String name, String value) {
  StringBuffer formOut = new StringBuffer();

  formOut.append("<input type=\"hidden\" name=\"")
          .append(name)
          .append("\" value=\"")
          .append(value)
          .append("\">\n");

  return (formOut.toString());
}

boolean isValidForm (HttpServletRequest req) {
  boolean valid = true;
  Enumeration need = fieldList.elements();

  while (need.hasMoreElements()) {
    formField field = (formField)need.nextElement();

    if (field.required) {
      String value = req.getParameter(field.name);
      if (value == null || value.equals("")) {
        valid = false;
      }
    }
  }

  return (valid);
}

String mailForm (HttpServletRequest req) throws JspException{
  StringBuffer message = new StringBuffer();

Enumeration fields = fieldList.elements();

  while (fields.hasMoreElements()) {
    formField field = (formField)fields.nextElement();
```

```
      message.append(field.name)
            .append(" : ")
            .append(req.getParameter(field.name))
            .append("\n");
   }

   // JavaMail here.
   Properties props = System.getProperties();
   props.put("mail.smtp.host", mailhost);
   Session emailsession = Session.getDefaultInstance(props,
       null);

   try {
     Message email = new MimeMessage(emailsession);
     email.setFrom(new InternetAddress(senderAddress));
     InternetAddress[] address = {
                    new InternetAddress(formRecipient) };
     email.setRecipients(Message.RecipientType.TO,address);
     email.setSubject(req.getServletPath());
     email.setSentDate(new Date());
     email.setHeader("X-Mailer","MailFormJava");
     email.setText(message.toString());
     Transport.send(email);
   } catch (MessagingException e) {
     throw new JspException (e.getMessage());
   }

   return (message.toString());
 }

%>


<%
  if (isValidForm(request)) {
    mailForm(request);
    // need to create a 'thanks for your comments' page
    response.sendRedirect("thanks.jsp");
  }
%>

<STYLE>
<!--
TD {
  font-family: Arial,Helvetica,sans-serif;
  font-size:10pt;
}
TABLE {
  background-color: #ffffcc;
}
-->
</STYLE>
```

```
<FORM ACTION="<%=request.getServletPath()%>" METHOD=POST>

<TABLE CELLPADDING=5 CELLSPACING=0 BORDER=0>
<%
  Enumeration fields = fieldList.elements();

  while (fields.hasMoreElements()) {

    formField field = (formField)fields.nextElement();
    String value = request.getParameter(field.name);

    if ( request.getParameter("Init") == null ||
        ( field.required && value.equals("") )
        ) {
%>
<TR>
<TD ALIGN=RIGHT><%= field.name %> : </TD>
<TD ALIGN=LEFT><%= displayField(field.name) %></TD>
</TR>
<%
    } else {
%>
<%= storeField(field.name, value) %>
<%
    }
  }
%>

<TR>
<TD COLSPAN=2 ALIGN=CENTER>
<INPUT TYPE=HIDDEN NAME="Init" VALUE="No">
<INPUT TYPE=SUBMIT VALUE="Send This">
</TD>
<TR>

</TABLE>

</FORM>
```

Script 8.2 is a simple form that includes Script 8.1, `mailForm.`
`jsp`.

Script 8.2
mailForm-wrapper.jsp

```
<!DOCTYPE HTML PUBLIC "-//W3C//DTD HTML 4.0 Final//EN">
<%@ page errorPage="errorPage.jsp" %>

<HEAD>
```

```
<TITLE> Stitch Magazine! Email Form </TITLE>
</HEAD>

<BODY>
A Generic Email Form<BR>
<jsp:include page="mailform.jsp" flush="true" />
</BODY>

</HTML>
```

The output of Script 8.2 should look similar to Figure 8–1.

8.1.4 Hidden Frames

Another means of getting a client to preserve and send state information is by using hidden frames. Implementing hidden

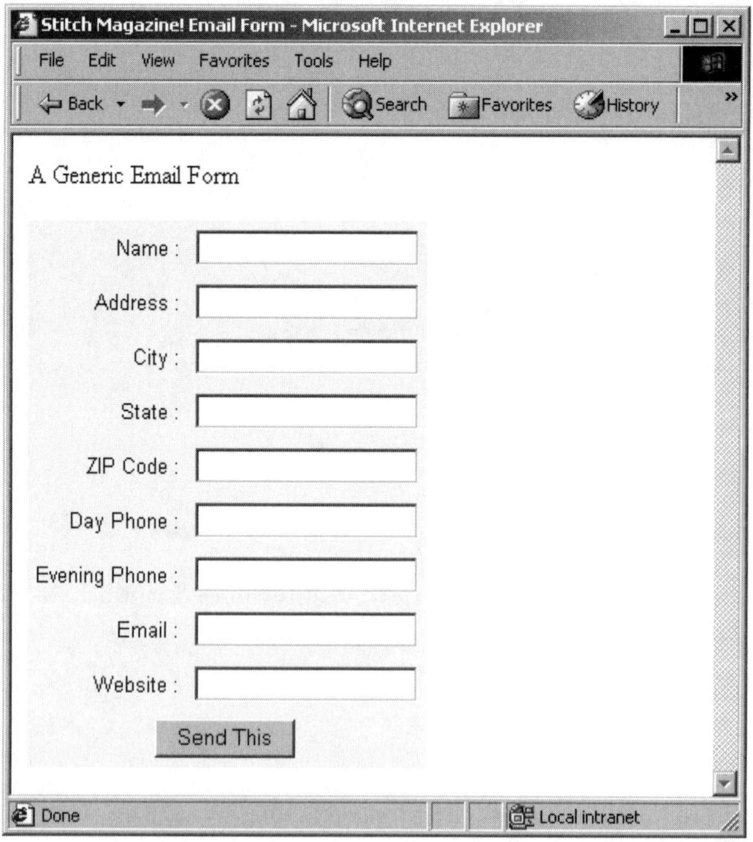

FIGURE 8–1 Mailform.jsp

frames is outside the scope of this book, but understanding how they work adds perspective to other methods.

By using a client-side scripting language and the browser's document object model (DOM), it is possible to retrieve and store data from any frame on a browser. It is also possible to create frames that are not seen by the user. Combining these two ideas allows a page author to create a hidden frame that can be used by the developer as a "scratch-pad" to add and remove information as needed.

Using hidden frame fields results in an extremely flexible way of preserving state. Unfortunately, not all browsers may support hidden frames. Browsers that support hidden frames often behave differently.

Overall, getting hidden frames to work properly can be a complex combination of client-side and server-side programming that can quickly become daunting and overwhelming.

8.1.5 URL Rewriting

State information can also be preserved by dynamically changing the URL that a user might click on. There are several ways that a URL can be modified and used to include extra information about a transaction.

State information can be put into the URL as standard HTTP GET parameters; for example:

```
http://www.javadesktop.com/catalog?category=books
```

The same general idea can be applied using a custom separator that is recognized by the server, but is different from the standard HTTP GET separator.

```
http://www.javadesktop.com/catalog;category=books
```

Alternatively, path information can be parsed by indicating a real page and a separate parameter; for example:

```
http://www.javadesktop.com/catalog/books
```

where `catalog` is the page and `books` is the parameter.

Ultimately, URL rewriting has similar advantages and disadvantages to using hidden form fields. One advantage is that URL rewriting can change information that does not reside within a form. Additionally, when used with a Session ID, less data is transferred with each transaction. Unfortunately, URL rewriting is significantly more complex to implement.

URLs are limited in length, so URL rewriting can be limited in the amount of information it can include. This is where Session IDs tend to become extremely important. Most URL rewriting in use will add only one parameter, a Session ID.

8.1.6 Cookies

Cookies are undoubtedly the most efficient and effective way to store state. In fact, all of the previously listed methods are attempts at using pre-existing facilities in new ways to preserve state. Cookies are the only method that was expressly designed from the ground up for preserving information about the state of a client.

Cookies can be set to store name/value pairs that might be needed to store state. Several cookies can be set to create a whole "picture" of the entire session. The actual details of setting, getting, and destroying cookies were discussed in Chapters 6, "Retrieving Information," and 7, "Sending Information."

In normal usage, it's unusual to store many cookies on a client. More likely, a cookie is sent that contains a Session ID or some other piece of information that uniquely identifies the client. Each time the browser sends a request, the cookie gets sent along with that request, allowing the server to maintain the information it needs to preserve state.

◆ 8.2 The HttpSession API

The actual work of managing sessions using a Session ID is a complex task. It involves generating unique keys that must be encoded properly, storing data transactions, and expiring sessions that are too old. Then notable parts from each transaction need to be stored in some internal database and be readily available when given the Session ID key.

Fortunately, there are methods built into the JSP API that will manage sessions. The API takes almost all the complexities of handling sessions and makes them into an elegant interface that is simple to implement.

8.2.1 The Basics

Session tracking begins with the server generating a unique ID for the user. The server then either sets a cookie or uses URL rewriting to store the Session ID. Most often, cookies will be used, but URL rewriting can be utilized (for sites that don't want to use cookies). Many JSP engines are intelligent in that they will first attempt to set a cookie and then revert to URL rewriting if cookies are not enabled on the client browser.

Next, a new instance of HttpSession is created. The new HttpSession object is accessible by using the Session ID as a key value. As long as the client returns the proper key, this same instance of the HttpSession object becomes accessible. If there are requests from multiple users, each will have their own HttpSession object, which will be accessible from only their own request.

The HttpSession object actually serves as a container that can be used to store or retrieve information. This object can store any number of other pieces of information. In fact, anything that extends java.lang.Object can be placed into the HttpSession object. This means that even more abstract data, including I/O streams and database connections, can be placed in the object and associated with a particular user.

ESSENTIAL NOTE: SESSION ID
The concept of a key begins to materialize as the amount of information kept about an HTTP connection increases. A Session ID is a single value that represents a key to a collection of state information kept on the server.

When a client presents this key, the server knows which collection of state data to use. The server is tracking the actual state of the transactions as long as the client preserves the key.

Session IDs have a number of advantages that stem from the fact that most of the data is kept on the server and does not have to be sent to the client. The bandwidth between transactions is reduced since the state data does not have to be sent back and forth with each transaction. In addition, there is increased security because only the session key is required to be passed between the client and the server.

8.2.2 Using the Session Object

By default, JSP has session tracking enabled and a new HttpSession object is instantiated for each new client automatically. There is nothing special that the JSP author needs to do to enable session tracking. In fact, actually disabling session tracking requires explicitly turning it off by setting the page directive session attribute to false.

```
<%@ page session="false" %>
```

The JSP engine exposes the `HttpSession` object to the JSP author through the implicit `session` object. Since this object is already provided to the JSP author, the author can immediately begin storing and retrieving data from the object without any initialization or `getSession()`.

There are a number of methods that can be used from the `session` object. The most important and most used methods are the ones directly related to storing and retrieving data.

ESSENTIAL NOTE: NEW SESSIONS

Java servlet programmers will need to take particular note that session tracking is set up by the JSP engine automatically. There is no need to go through the process of creating a new session.

---

void session.putValue(String key, Object value)

`putValue()` is a fairly simple method that does the actual work of storing the value object within the `session` object. The object specified as the value will get stored under the string `key`.

Only one value may be stored at any particular name. Using `putValue()` on a key name that already contains an object will simply overwrite the old data without any warning.

Object session.getValue(String name)

`getValue()` is the complement of `putValue()`. This method retrieves data from the `session` object. If there is no corresponding value for the key, then a null value is returned.

Since the return value from this method is an `Object`, it will typically need to be cast into the correct object type. For example:
```
String value = (String)session.getvalue(name);
```

void session.removeValue(String name)

This method is used to remove a value from the `session` object. It is important to note that a value cannot be removed by setting the value to null (`session.putValue(name, null)`); in fact, this will throw `nullPointerException`.

String[] session.getValueNames()

This method returns a `String` array that contains the key name of each entry stored in the `session` object. Using this method allows for listing or "sniffing" the session data.

ESSENTIAL NOTE: SESSION **OBJECT**

The session object uses method names that resemble the methods used by the collection classes (HashMap, etc.), but instead closely resembles the cookie object. This being the case, there are some things to be particularly wary of.

First off, the session object will always require a String for the key name. Other classes extended from java.lang.Object are not usable as key names.

But most notably, unlike the collection classes, neither the key names nor the values of session object may contain a null value. If a null is found, then the page will throw a nullPointerException at execution-time and will not complete properly.

Script 8.3 shows an addition to the previous example of Script 8.1. The wrapper framework that contains the included files is shown in Script 8.4.

The example creates the debug page that is included in the framework from the previous mailForm.jsp example. This debug mode is transparent until the URL includes a debug parameter set to true (e.g., ?debug=true).

Once debug mode is activated that state is stored in the client's session. Thereafter, all the pages that include debug.jsp will see the request and session data until the session expires. Since there are no changes to the standard session, this will typically mean a certain time period of inactivity, or a closing of the browser.

Script 8.3
debug.jsp

```
<%@ page import ="java.util.*" %>

<%!
  String debugDump (HttpSession session) {
    StringBuffer data = new StringBuffer();

    String names[] = session.getValueNames();

    if (names != null) {

      for (int item=0; item < names.length; item++) {
        data.append("  ")
          .append(names[item])

          .append(" :   ")
          .append(session.getValue(names[item]))
```

```
                         .append("<BR>\n");
            }
         }

      return (data.toString());
   }

   String debugDump (HttpServletRequest request) {
      StringBuffer data = new StringBuffer();

      Enumeration reqdata = request.getParameterNames();
      while(reqdata.hasMoreElements()) {
         String name = (String)reqdata.nextElement();
         String values[]
            = request.getParameterValues(name);

         if (values != null) {

            for (int item=0; item < values.length; item++) {
               data.append("  ")
                   .append(name)
                   .append(" [")
                   .append(item)
                   .append("] ")
                   .append(" : ")
                   .append(values[item])
                   .append("<BR>\n");
            }
         }
      }

      return (data.toString());
   }
%>
<%
   String setDebug = request.getParameter("debug");
   if (setDebug != null) {
      session.putValue("debug", setDebug);
   }

   String debug = (String)session.getValue("debug");

   if (debug != null && debug.equals("true")) {
%>
<STYLE>
<!--
.debugtext {
   color: #000000; font-size: 7pt;
   font-family: courier,serif;
   font-weight: 600;
}
```

```
-->
</STYLE>


<TABLE BORDER=1 CELLSPACING=0 CELLPADDING=0><TR><TD>
<TABLE BORDER=0 CELLSPACING=0 CELLPADDING=4>

<TR><TD CLASS="debugtext">
DEBUG DATA
</TD></TR>

<TR><TD CLASS="debugtext">
SESSION:<BR>
<%= debugDump(session) %><BR>
</TD></TR>

<TR><TD CLASS="debugtext">
REQUEST:<BR>
<%= debugDump(request) %><BR>
</TD></TR>

</TABLE>
</TD></TR></TABLE>

<%
    }
%>
```

Script 8.4 shows a simple JSP page that includes a form and Script 8.3, debug.jsp.

Script 8.4
mailForm-wrapper2.jsp

```
<!DOCTYPE HTML PUBLIC "-//W3C//DTD HTML 4.0 Final//EN">
<%@ page errorPage="errorPage.jsp" %>

<HEAD>
<TITLE> Stitch Magazine! Email Form </TITLE>
</HEAD>

<BODY>
<jsp:include page="debug.jsp" flush="true" />
A Generic Email Form<BR>
<jsp:include page="mailform.jsp" flush="true" />
</BODY>

</HTML>
```

The new mailform-wrapper.jsp with debug.jsp included would look like Figure 8–2.

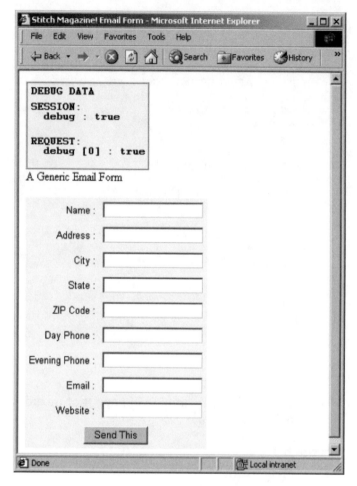

FIGURE 8–2 Mail Form with Debugging Information

In theory, the `mailform.jsp` example shown in Script 8.1 could also be reworked to use session tracking instead of hidden form fields. But this would probably become more complicated because the end results would need to be ultimately sent through an HTML form.

8.2.3 The Life of a Session

Sessions are intended to preserve state between transactions; they are not designed to last. If a session is ever lost, then its data is irretrievable, regardless of whether it was by the intention of the JSP author or by the server crashing.

While sessions are reliable, they are really not intended for the long-term storage of data. Long-term storage of user data should be achieved by using some form of authentication and an external data source, such as a database or file. Sessions still play a very important role in identifying a user and associating the user with their data. In fact, a common tactic is to use the session as a database cache of sorts.

Sessions keep a series of time stamps to indicate different things. One use of these time stamps is to automatically expire sessions that have been inactive for too long. The default before a session is removed is usually configured in the JSP engine. Of course, the JSP author can remove a particular session at any time.

ESSENTIAL NOTE: SESSION MEMORY SPACE

Sessions are an extremely powerful and useful feature, but it's good to bear in mind the memory footprint when putting objects into sessions.

Since session data lasts for a fixed period of time and the session can store large amounts of data, it is relatively easy to saturate memory on a high-traffic site. As an example, consider a site that keeps sessions for 1 hour, gets 500 clients per hour, and stores an average of 40K bytes per client. This winds up consuming 20MB of RAM (albeit some of that may get swapped to disk).

Reducing data size per client or reducing the session keep-alive time will reduce the overall memory footprint. But the opposite holds true as well; increasing either of these increases the memory footprint.

There are two simple things that can reduce memory size. First, be sure to remove specific data from a session when it is no longer useful. Second, don't let sessions hang around when they are known to be closed; explicitly invalidate these sessions.

The session API provides the JSP author with a series of methods that help to check and control the life cycle of a session.

```
int session.getMaxInactiveInterval()
```

```
void session.setMaxInactiveInterval
(int interval)
```

getMaxInactiveInterval() returns the number of seconds that need to pass before a session will expire. setMaxInactive-Interval() allows the JSP author to change the amount of time before a particular session will expire.

```
long session.getCreationTime()
long session.getLastAccessedTime()
```

`getCreationTime()` returns the time that the session was created. `getLastAccessedTime()` returns the last time the session was used. Both of these methods return the time as the number of seconds since *epoch* (12 midnight, Jan. 1, 1970).

```
void session.invalidate()
```

`invalidate()` simply destroys the existing session. Once a session has been invalidated, there is no way to regain it.

This method is particularly useful in creating "logout" methods. It can also be useful in sweeping out really old sessions that might occur from external applications that reconnect regularly and never allow the session to expire.

```
boolean session.isNew()
```

Allows the JSP author a means to determine if this is a new session. This method returns `true` if this is a newly created session.

```
string session.getId()
```

Returns the unique string identifier for the session.

```
Enumeration session.getIds()
```

Returns an enumeration of all the currently valid Session IDs.

ESSENTIAL NOTE: SESSION ID SECURITY RISK
It's important to point out that giving out the Session ID itself presents a security risk. Knowing another user's Session ID might allow a mischievous user to piggyback on another user's session and effectively become that user. In most of these cases, the safest tactic is simply to never display the Session ID back to the user.

◆ 8.3 Sessions and Identity

The concept of state implies client identity. As any site becomes more complex and dependent on state, the complexity of the identity of the client grows in scale. Some type of authentication is needed to identify each user, and since state is maintainable it is also possible to manage a login process using the `session` object.

The next example is a session-based login system. This will allow for page-based access by including a small chunk of code at the top of any "secure" page. If a client tries to get to a secure page without having logged in, it is prompted for information.

The next example requires several components: Scripts 8.5, 8.6, and 8.7. Script 8.5 shows the JSP file that actually checks whether a user has logged in. It needs to be included using a `page` directive (using `<%@ include file="..." %>`), because it needs to modify the HTTP response headers to redirect requests to a login page. It should be included near the top of any JSP page, generally where the user's identity is important.

Script 8.5
`confirmLogin.jsp`

```
<%
   String login = (String)session.getValue("login");

   if ( login == null ) {
     StringBuffer loginpoint = new StringBuffer();

     loginpoint.append(request.getScheme())
               .append("://")
               .append(request.getServerName())
               .append(request.getRequestURI());

     session.putValue("loginpoint", loginpoint.toString());

     StringBuffer loginpage = new StringBuffer();

     loginpage.append(request.getScheme())
              .append("://")
              .append(request.getServerName())
              .append("/")
              .append("login.jsp");

     response.sendRedirect(loginpage.toString());
   }
%>
```

Script 8.6 shows the heart of the login system. This page is presented whenever anyone tries to access a restricted page without having the proper tokens. When they have logged in, they are given the proper identification tokens.

Script 8.6
`login.jsp`

```
<%@ page errorPage="errorPage.jsp" %>
```

```
<%
  String login = (String)request.getParameter("loginname");

  if (login == null || login.equals("")) {
%>
<!DOCTYPE HTML PUBLIC "-//W3C//DTD HTML 4.0 Final//EN">
<HEAD>
<TITLE>Login Page</TITLE>
<STYLE>
<!--
font.loginhead {
  font-family: Arial,Helvetica,sans-serif;
  font-size:12pt; font-weight: 600; color: #000000;
}
font.loginform {
  font-family: Arial,Helvetica,sans-serif;
  font-size:10pt; font-weight: 600; color: #ffffff;
}
-->
</STYLE>
</HEAD>

<BODY>
<jsp:include page="debug.jsp" flush="true" />

<CENTER>
<FONT CLASS="loginhead">
LOGIN REQUIRED:
</FONT>
<BR>

<FORM NAME="loginform" METHOD=post>
<TABLE BGCOLOR=#990022 BORDER=0 CELLPADDING=5 CELLSPACING=0>

<TR><TD ALIGN=right>
<FONT CLASS="loginform">
Login Name:
</FONT>
</TD><TD ALIGN=left>
<FONT CLASS="loginform">
<INPUT TYPE=text NAME="loginname" SIZE=10>
</FONT>
</TD></TR>

<TR><TD ALIGN=right>
<FONT CLASS="loginform">
Password:
</FONT>
</TD><TD ALIGN=left>
<FONT CLASS="loginform">
<INPUT TYPE=password NAME="loginpassword" SIZE=10>
```

```
</FONT>
</TD></TR>

<TR><TD COLSPAN=2 ALIGN=center>
<FONT CLASS="loginform">
<INPUT TYPE=SUBMIT VALUE="Login">
</FONT>
</TD></TR>
</TABLE>

</FORM>
</CENTER>

</BODY>
</HTML>
<%
  } else {
  /*
This should check against a database to make sure the password is
    correct, and retrieve user data. Right now, it doesn't.
*/

    session.putValue("login", login);
    session.setMaxInactiveInterval(600);

    String loginpoint
      = (String)session.getValue("loginpoint");
    if (loginpoint == null) {
      StringBuffer defaultpoint = new StringBuffer();
      defaultpoint.append(request.getScheme())
                  .append("://")
                  .append(request.getServerName())
                  .append("/");

      loginpoint = defaultpoint.toString();
    } else {
      session.removeValue("loginpoint");
    }

    response.sendRedirect(loginpoint);
  }
%>
```

The output of Script 8.6 should look like Figure 8–3.

Script 8.7 shows the logout page. Logging out the user could be accomplished by invalidating the session, which would create a whole new session. Preserved information outside of the login process might also be desired, so the key is simply removed. Finally, the user is redirected to a location that does not require a login.

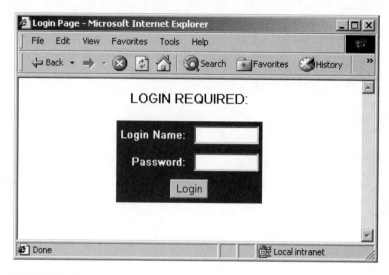

FIGURE 8–3 login.jsp

Script 8.7
logout.jsp

```
<%
session.removeValue("login");

/*
  To use logout by destroying the session, uncomment the
  line below.
*/
//session.invalidate();

  StringBuffer logout = new StringBuffer();

  logout.append(request.getScheme())
        .append("://")
        .append(request.getServerName())
        .append("/");

  response.sendRedirect(logout.toString());
%>
```

Unfortunately, until some form of a database has been introduced, this login system only functions as a means of asking for a name. Later, as directory service or database concepts are introduced, this example will get reworked to include true password authentication and preference information.

Another drawback to the above example is that the login system is fairly passive. It doesn't really have an entry point; it only uses hooks to insert it into other pages. As a mechanism to make this concept work, a navigation bar will be introduced.

Script 8.7 is the navigation bar itself. It has been implemented in a way that will leave it open to later expansion. For the time being, it works using fairly static options. Like the login method, the navigation bar will be expanded upon later, when database access has been discussed.

Script 8.7
navbar.jsp

```
<%@ page import ="java.util.*" %>

<%!
  class tab {
     String tabname;
     String location;

     tab (String name, String value) {
        this.tabname = name;
        this.location = value;
     }
  }
%>

<%
  Vector leftnavbar = new Vector();
  Vector rightnavbar = new Vector();

 leftnavbar.add(new tab("Main", "/"));
 leftnavbar.add(new tab("Maillists", "/maillists.jsp"));

  rightnavbar.add(new tab("Logout", "/logout.jsp"));
  rightnavbar.add(new tab("Preferences", "/prefs.jsp"));
%>

<STYLE>
<!--
td.navbar {
  background-color: #990022;
  margin: 1px; padding: 1px; border: 1px;
}
font.navtext {
  font-family: arial,helvetica,sans-serif;
  font-weight: 600; text-decoration: none;
  font-size: 10pt; color: #ffffff;
}
```

```
-->
</STYLE>

<TABLE WIDTH=100% BORDER=0 CELLPADDING=0 CELLSPACING=0>
<TR>
<TD ALIGN=LEFT CLASS="navbar">

<TABLE CELLPADDING=3 CELLSPACING=2 BORDER=0>
<TR>
<%

  Enumeration lefttabs = leftnavbar.elements();

  while (lefttabs.hasMoreElements()) {
    tab current = (tab)lefttabs.nextElement();

%>
<TD>
<A HREF="<%=current.location%>">
<FONT CLASS="navtext">
<%=current.tabname%>
</FONT>
</A>
</TD>

<%
  }
%>
</TR>
</TABLE>
</TD>

<TD ALIGN=RIGHT CLASS="navbar">
<TABLE CELLPADDING=5 CELLSPACING=2 BORDER=0>
<TR>
<%

  Enumeration righttabs = rightnavbar.elements();

  while (righttabs.hasMoreElements()) {
    tab current = (tab)righttabs.nextElement();

%>
<TD>
<A HREF="<%=current.location%>">
<FONT CLASS="navtext">
<%=current.tabname%>
</FONT>
</A>
</TD>
```

```
<%
   }
%>
</TR>
</TABLE>
</TD>

</TR>
</TABLE>

<BR><BR>
```

Script 8.8 shows how the framework would change to include the new additions to the site.

Script 8.8
index-navbar.jsp

```
<%@ page errorPage="errorPage.jsp" %>
<%@ include file="confirmLogin.jsp" %>

<!DOCTYPE HTML PUBLIC "-//W3C//DTD HTML 4.0 Final//EN">

<HEAD>
<TITLE> Stitch Magazine! </TITLE>
</HEAD>

<BODY>
<jsp:include page="debug.jsp" flush="true" />
<jsp:include page="navbar.jsp" flush="true" />
</BODY>
</HTML>
```

8.3.1 Security Concerns

As identity becomes more important, potential problems from mistaken or stolen identities increase. So, some system should be put in place to protect the user's access.

Fortunately, because JSP pages are compiled and executed on the server, many traditional security concerns are avoided entirely. Again, keep in mind that the actual data about the session is stored on the server and is not given to the client. This gives sessions a layer of security. Information stored in a session like a login token is never passed back to the user, and never requested from the user, so there is really nothing that can be spoofed or forged here.

However, it's extremely important to realize that this does not protect JSP pages from evildoers. There are still a number of major considerations in creating secure pages, including the following:

- It is usually a bad idea to print a Session ID. This is not useful information for most clients. It might be useful in doing debugging work, but it's worth always sending through `application.log()`, just in case something doesn't work as planned.
- Never send the entire list of Session IDs (using `getIds()`) through `out`. Having another user's Session ID will allow a user to piggyback with another user's session.
- Of course, there is not enough that can be said for requiring clients to select decent passwords. Encryption technology today is so powerful that it's common to have compromises from brute-force guessing.
- Always use a secure server (SSL) for any page that on which the user needs to type in a password. This will help prevent people from getting their passwords "sniffed."

There is no way a full list of all the potential security issues could be printed here. It is beyond the scope of this book. For additional information, there are a number of great resources available on the Web, and there are several very good books on the topic.

◆ 8.4 Recap

The JSP specification authors understood the value of including a session-tracking API in JSP. It effectively adds state information to HTTP. This is a key factor in creating complex Web applications and prepares JSP for bigger and better tasks. The next chapter, "Using JavaBeans," describes how to connect these sessions to enterprise-class Java applications.

9 Using JavaBeans

chapter

IN THIS CHAPTER

- The Component Model
- JavaBeans
- Components and Component Frameworks
- Enterprise JavaBeans
- Recap

Previous examples have made extensive use of embedding JSP using the `include` *action (* `<jsp:include />`*) and the* `include` *directive (* `<%@ include %>` *). Each of these methods works in slightly different ways, but both present significant scalability problems.*

The `include` *directive (* `<%@ include %>` *) effectively inserts code in-line. This can create potential namespace collisions or significant problems with overlapping declarations. The* `include` *action (* `<jsp:include />` *) inserts the output of a second JSP page into the original page, which can create problems in trying to share data or when the secondary JSP does something erratic.*

For each of these methods, there is also no standardized interface. Each developer creates their own classes and methods, each with its own syntax and signature. Finding a second developer that can easily work with another developer's inline code relies heavily on documentation, comments, and the "like-minded-ness" of developers that may not exist.

These approaches are also not conducive to separating business logic from presentation. One the most powerful abilities in JSP is its ability to separate the hard code from the presentation of the page into two distinct entities.

◆ 9.1 The Component Model

In 1798, the U.S. Government decided to end its reliance on foreign countries to purchase army muskets. Eli Whitney, made famous for his invention of the cotton gin, secured a contract to produce 10,000 army muskets.

The problem was there were only a handful of skilled machinists in the early American republic. To solve this problem, Whitney invented something far more important than a machine. He invented a system that would permit anyone to create a product that would be just as good as one made by a highly trained machinist.

Whitney based his system on interchangeable parts, and called his solution the "Uniformity System." He later demonstrated that randomly selected individual parts would fit together to create a working musket. Until then, every rifle had been made by hand from stock to barrel. No parts of one gun would fit into another. More important than filling his order, Eli Whitney had created the component model.

Computer programming begins to embrace the component model with the development of an "object model" in object-oriented programming languages such as C++ and Java. While the object model breathed life into the development of complex applications, its distribution was still limited to language libraries and APIs. Joining two complex libraries still takes the skill and finesse of someone well versed in the language and methods of the APIs.

More recently, another model has been applied on top of the object model. This newer model draws on the best advantages of the object model, but it also implements the idea of the interface. Under this new model, a packaged set of code is created that communicates with other components through a set of standardized methods called interfaces. In this "component model," plugging together interfaces of different components creates applications.

Using a component architecture grants a powerful level of code reusability and interchangeability. Components should behave the same way everywhere they go and can be "plugged-in" wherever or whenever needed. The component also provides an extremely powerful ability to abstract business logic from presentation. Designers continue to work on presentation, yet draw upon powerful tools without understanding the programming behind them. A developer who specializes in a very specific technology can develop a component without going over the intricate details of how it works, and still share it with his coworkers and teammates.

9.1.1 The Component Model for JSP

Like many other aspects of JSP, a JSP page uses the component model that is built right into the underlying Java platform. The JavaBean component architecture was introduced in Java 1.1 and further refined in Java 1.2. JSP is designed to take full advantage of this JavaBean component architecture.

JavaBeans were originally designed to be graphical components in a graphical user interface (GUI). Fortunately, the architecture and design pattern used by JavaBeans does not really lock them into any specific application model. Even before JSP started to support JavaBeans, they were already beginning to be used to create non-graphical, data-centric components.

By using the component architecture that is already built into the language, JSP can leverage a large pool of existing JavaBean components. While many of these data-centric JavaBeans may not have originally been intended for JSP, their component architecture will allow them to plug right in.

Unfortunately, since JavaBeans were used for user interface components for so long, the majority of the current documentation on JavaBeans refers to them as graphical widgets. These JavaBeans really are the same as graphical component JavaBeans and all the concepts remain the same.

◆ 9.2 JavaBeans

A JavaBean is basically a standard Java class that adheres to a set of fairly simple design and naming conventions. A JavaBean defines its exported methods and objects in a standardized naming convention that can be easily derived by the calling application. This provides a programmatic entry (interface) into the JavaBean without understanding how the JavaBean works internally.

There are actually no requirements for a JavaBean to extend or superclass any other object. Any class that follows the JavaBean conventions is a JavaBean. So, the true essence of creating new JavaBeans is really a programming paradigm more than calling specific API methods.

The JavaBean API does provide a simple container class that knows how to expose these properties in special ways to create interfaces. But this is really not relevant to the JSP author or Java-Bean developer. The JavaBeans API really applies to applications that "handle" JavaBeans, such as "bean-boxes" or the JSP engine itself.

9.2.1 JavaBean Conventions

By using standard design and naming conventions, a JavaBean can be used by applications that do not understand the under-lying logic of the JavaBean. Adhering to specific semantics and rules allows applications like JSP to analyze the classes and methods that are available to derive the method invocations and properties that are available.

These conventions contain specific requirements on how the class must be designed. Fortunately, these design requirements are fairly straightforward and resemble "good: object-oriented programming methodologies.

There are three design requirements for a JavaBean. First, the constructor needs to accept no parameters. Second, all access to the JavaBean is done through these specially defined accessor methods. And finally, a JavaBean needs to be distributed in a JAR file in a special way.

ESSENTIAL NOTE: JAVABEAN NAMING CONVENTIONS
The specification for JavaBeans does not require any specific convention for naming classes. They can be named whatever the JavaBean developer believes is most appropriate. However, there is an informal class naming convention that is used to help other developers more easily identify JavaBeans.

Typically, a JavaBean will usually follow Java's standard naming convention of beginning each word section with a capital letter. In addition, the JavaBean will usually have a class name that ends in the word "`Bean`" (for example, "`LdapBean`", "`ClockBean`", etc.).

THE CONSTRUCTOR

By definition, a JavaBean is required to have a constructor that is instantiated with no parameters. This makes sense, considering that the calling application may not know how the JavaBean actually functions. It would be nearly impossible for the calling application to derive an understanding of the specific instantia-tion parameters that might be required.

While all JavaBeans require a constructor with no parameters, it is certainly possible to overload the constructor with several signatures. This is not uncommon for classes that have been converted from non-JavaBean classes into JavaBeans. But, the default `<jsp:useBean>` tag will only actually use the constructor that has no parameters.

Java also supports classes without constructors. When this is the case, the Java compiler creates a constructor that contains no parameters and initializes no values. This means that a Java-Bean could even be an empty class file and still remain valid; for example, this is a valid JavaBean:

```
public class EmptyBean {}
```

PROPERTIES AND ACCESSOR METHODS

When working with a JavaBean, every aspect of the JavaBean that is exposed is called a property. A property is really just an external representation of the internal state of the JavaBean.

For each property, there will be accessor methods that define interaction with the property. These accessor methods either set a value or get a value from a specific property. The JavaBean should never have its internal state accessed directly, so every modifiable aspect of the JavaBean should have accessor methods.

Most frequently, a property will have accessor methods that allow setting and getting a value. However, there is no specific requirement that a property must have both of these accessor methods; it could have just one. Some properties may not allow a property to be set, so no accessor method would be available.

Accessor methods are created using a common naming format. Once again, this is to allow information about the Java-Bean to be derived without explicit knowledge of the JavaBean.

The methods used for retrieving data are called *getter* methods and follow this format:

```
public {Object-Type} get{Property} ()
```

The complements to these are the *setter* methods that allow for placing data into a property. The *setter* methods follow this format:

```
public void set{Property} ({Object-Type})
```

JavaBeans also provide an additional accessor method that returns a Boolean value. This accessor method is known as a

Boolean getter method. It is useful for checking state or other flags in the JavaBean.

```
public boolean is{Property} ()
```

VISIBILITY

Normally, the visibility of methods and variables is left open to the developer. However, the JavaBean requires that all accessor methods be declared as `public` methods. The JSP container will only be able to identify properties that are `public` accessor methods, so other non-`public` accessor methods will not be available to JSP pages.

The visibility of internal objects and methods within the JavaBean is still open to the option of the developer. But since the JavaBean is intended as a means of encapsulating logic, it really doesn't make sense to have anything public besides the accessor methods.

Serious consideration should be given to any object within a JavaBean that is declared as `public`. Usually only the constructor and accessor methods of the JavaBean should be `public`. Most other objects should probably be `protected` or `private` and have their properties exposed through `public` accessor methods. This will keep the users of a JavaBean accessing it through the standard interfaces and prevent potential problems that might occur if the internal implementation of the JavaBean changes.

9.2.2 JavaBean Examples

Script 9.1 shows a JavaBean that acts as a simple counter. This JavaBean doesn't do anything incredibly interesting, but it does illustrate some of the requirements of a JavaBean.

The constructor takes no parameters and still initializes the variables that are needed for the JavaBean. In this particular case, the bean has only one property, `count`, which is accessed through a getter method for that property.

Script 9.1
SimpleCountingBean.java

```
public class SimpleCountingBean {
  private int count;

  public SimpleCountingBean() {
    count = 0;
```

```
    }

    public int getCount() {
      count++;
      return count;
    }
}
```

ESSENTIAL NOTE: USING JAVABEANS

Normally with JSP, one has the luxury of not having to compile classes because a JSP page is handled automatically by the JSP engine. This is not the case for a JavaBean. The JavaBean needs to be compiled using the standard Java compiler (`javac`).

The compiled JavaBean is really just a new class, so it needs to be made available the way any other class would be. When the JSP engine goes to compile a JSP page that contains a JavaBean, the JavaBean's class is essentially "`import`"ed automatically by the JSP engine.

From the perspective of JSP, this means that the first class in the server's CLASSPATH matches the value defined by the 'class=' attribute in the `jsp:useBean` tag. So, any individual .class file that could be imported and used as a JavaBean will be used as a JavaBean without complaint. Simply being in the CLASSPATH will allow a JavaBean to behave exactly as anyone would expect.

Script 9.2 shows another simple JavaBean, but this one is a bit more complicated. This JavaBean actually represents a user in an address book system. This JavaBean has both getter and setter methods that allow it to actually act as a data repository for information about the user.

Script 9.2
UserInfoBean.java

```
    import java.util.*;

    public class Contact {
      private String name=null;
      private String phone=null;
      private String email=null;

      public Contact() { }

      public String getName() {
        return this.name;
```

```
   }

   public void setName(String myName) {
     this.name = myName;
   }

   public String getPhone() {
     return this.phone;
   }

   public void setPhone(String myPhone) {
     this.phone = myPhone;
   }

   public String getEmail() {
     return this.email;
   }

   public void setEmail(String myEmail) {
     this.email = myEmail;
   }

}
```

9.2.3 Other Requirements

There are some additional requirements in the JavaBeans specification that are part of the more traditional form of JavaBeans. However, the JSP engine should not normally require these.

These requirements should be strictly adhered to if the goal is to create fully qualified JavaBeans. If the goal is simply to make a JavaBean that works with JSP, then these are still useful and recommended, but are not required.

PACKAGING

It looks like a JavaBean, and it behaves like a JavaBean, so is it a JavaBean? Well, it might not be a JavaBean as defined by the JavaBeans specification, even though most people wouldn't notice the difference. Technically, it is not a JavaBean until the new class is placed into a JAR file that includes a specific manifest option. Each class file that is a JavaBean needs to be marked with the 'Java-Bean: true' attribute in the manifest file.

Specific examples in how to use these commands will be shown later as the JavaBean examples are packaged.

USING THE SERIALIZABLE INTERFACE

Earlier in the chapter, it was said that JavaBeans do not need to implement any particular interface, and that is still true for Java-Beans used within JSP. However, the JavaBeans specification actually requires that all JavaBeans implement the `serializable` interface.

Serialization allows JavaBeans to be saved to disk, sent across a network, or written into a database. Later, the same JavaBean can be reread and restored to its state at the time that it was stored.

Serialization turns an object, such as a JavaBean, into a stream of data that resembles a byte array. This data contains representations of the raw data types and all the raw data that is currently contained in the JavaBean. This data can then be put just about anywhere that a byte array output stream can go. Later, when the data needs to be reconstituted, it undergoes a reversing process that de-serializes the data back into the same data structures.

Serialized JavaBeans can be extremely powerful in storing data. Rather than storing discrete data segments in a database, the actual JavaBean can be stored and restored using serialization. Consider an eCommerce order from a customer. Traditionally, the data would consist of a series of elements from a series of database tables, which can be difficult and expensive to reconstruct. Alternatively, if the order was all done as a JavaBean, it would be serialized and stored, and reconstructing it would be as simple as de-serializing the JavaBean.

The `serializable` interface also lets the developer create a JavaBean that is pre-configured. This bypasses the "empty constructor" requirement to some degree by creating the new Java-Bean using a template. When the `<jsp:useBean>` tag is given the `beanName` attribute, it will instantiate a new bean from a serialized file (`*.ser`) that matches the class name of the JavaBean. If there is no serialized file, then JSP will create new JavaBean using the empty constructor.

Creating a JavaBean that can be serialized simply involves implementing the `serializable` interface; but, making serialization behave properly is a discussion that is beyond the scope of this book.

9.2.4 Beyond the Requirements

So far everything that has been discussed about JavaBeans has been an aspect of the required conventions. JavaBeans also provide a number of other convenience functions that can optionally be used by the JSP developer.

INDEXED PROPERTIES

Normal properties are restricted to a single value only. There is an additional type of property that supports multiple values, where all the values must be of the same data type. These are called indexed properties, and they deal with arrays of data.

Indexed properties have *getter* and *setter* methods like normal properties, but there are methods for each that retrieve the entire array or a single value from that array.

The first set handles the entire array, getting or setting the array through a single accessor method as follows:

```
public {Object-Type}[] get{Property} ()
public void set{Property} ({Object-Type}[])
```

The other type of accessor methods for indexed properties refer to a specific index within the array, setting or getting a single value as follows:

```
public {Object-Type} get{Property} (int)
public set{Property} (int, {Object-Type})
```

9.2.5 Introspection

So far, there is no common method or base class for an application to use to derive information about a JavaBean. But somehow, an application using a JavaBean knows what accessor methods and properties are available. It is probably time to talk briefly about this process and the underlying technologies.

When a JavaBean is instantiated, the JavaBean container starts by going through a process called "introspection." The introspection process collects data from several sources. Most of the information obtained comes from another process called "reflection," which simply scans the method signatures of the class. Next, introspection matches the known naming conventions for a JavaBean and builds a list of accessor methods.

Finally, once all the data has come back, the process will make some decisions about how accessor methods and properties will actually be exposed. The process of simply looking at method signatures essentially defines the properties and accessor methods.

OVERRIDING INTROSPECTION

JavaBeans also provide a mechanism to specifically override introspection. This is actually a combination of a class and an interface that needs to be defined. First, a class that is prefixed by

'BeanInfo' needs to be created, and the class needs to implement the `java.beans.BeanInfo` interface.

By using `BeanInfo`, a developer can explicitly change which internal method is connected to each accessor method or property. A developer can designate any arbitrary method to map across to a specific JavaBean property. This can be particularly useful when an existing non-JavaBean class needs to be converted into a JavaBean, but still needs to retain the original method name.

Implementing a `BeanInfo` class can get somewhat complicated, and most of the features are designed for use in applications that actually handle JavaBeans, like visual JSP editors. While it is a bit beyond the scope of this book, a simple implementation framework is available at `java.beans.SimpleBeanInfo`.

9.2.6 Using a JavaBean in JSP

Everything up to this point has discussed the process of creating and changing actual JavaBeans, but there has been no discussion about using JavaBeans within JSP.

There was a lengthy discussion on the specific semantics of the tags `<jsp:useBean>`, `<jsp:getProperty>`, and `<jsp:set Property>`, including the valid signatures for each tag, in previous chapters.

ESSENTIAL NOTE: RECOMPILING JSP

When a JSP page is changed, it is automatically recompiled by the JSP engine. But, most JSP servers will not recompile a page if a Java-Bean was changed. If a JavaBean was changed and the JSP page should be recompiled, then the JSP engine will need to be told to re-compile the JSP page. This might be as easy as using a "touch" command to update the last-modified date of the file.

JSP TYPE CONVERSIONS

The JSP tags `<jsp:setProperty>` and `<jsp:getProperty>` deal with every value as a scalar; every value they receive is converted into a `String`. This is not a limitation created by the JavaBean, it is simply how the JSP engine handles these tags.

These tags automatically call the `toString()` method associated with the object just before the actual JavaBean is given the value or immediately after the value is received back. For primitive types, the data is converted using the corresponding object in the `java.lang.*.toString()` method (for example, a `double` uses `java.lang.Double.toString ()`).

Since this occurs in the layer just before the JavaBean, the actual methods that are requested will effectively have these signatures:

```
public String get{Property} ()
public void set{Property} (String n)
```

For example, Script 9.1 has a method that returns an `int`. In this case, when the JSP engine sees the tag `<jsp:getProperty name="counter" property="count">`, it behaves as if an accessor method was called that looks like this:

```
public String getCount()
```

AVOIDING JSP TYPE CONVERSIONS

It's possible to avoid the type conversions that occur in JSP by simply not using the standard tags `<jsp:getProperty>` and `<jsp:setProperty>`. The first and simplest way to avoid these problems is to use the JavaBean the same way a normal class would be used. In this case, the bean is still instantiated as a JavaBean using the `<jsp:useBean>` tag. The properties of the bean can be accessed by calling the accessor methods directly. For example:

```
<jsp:useBean id="pagecounter" class="SimpleCounterBean">
<%
   int count = pagecounter.getCount();
%>
```

Since this called the accessor method directly (without JSP interpreting the tag), it will actually return an `int`.

ESSENTIAL NOTE: NULLS AND PROPERTIES

In addition to converting the resulting values into a `String`, the `<jsp:setProperty>` and `<jsp:getProperty>` tags don't handle nulls very well under a large number of JSP engines.

If either of these tags is given a null as a value, or receives a null back from an accessor method, then an exception is thrown. This is probably not the behavior that would be expected.

This can either be avoided by changing the JavaBean or by calling the accessor methods directly.

An alternative method of avoiding JSP type conversions would be to create custom JSP tags that can handle the appropriate data types. A custom tag can be created to accept or return any type of data that might be needed. More information on creating custom tags is available in the next chapter.

THE SCOPE OF A JAVABEAN

JSP supports using JavaBeans under the same four different levels of scope that any page can have: `request`, `page`, `session`, and `application`. Each JavaBean is created with its own scope, independent of the page. This allows the JavaBean to actually have significantly different behaviors under different scopes. JavaBeans can outlive a page, or they can have a shorter lifespan than a page, depending on the context that is needed.

In fact, a JavaBean as simple as the one shown in Script 9.1 can have significantly different behaviors depending on its scope. While the `request` and `page` scopes would be pretty useless for this JavaBean (they would count then be discarded), using this JavaBean in the `session` scope would allow the counter to track how often a particular user requested a page up until his or her session expired. Used in the `application` scope, the counter would track how often a page was accessed by anyone since the server was last restarted.

JAVABEANS AND THREAD SAFETY

JavaBeans instantiate quite a few objects that are not inherently thread-safe. Since the JSP engine is a threaded environment, JavaBeans may have some problems that come about as a result of threading. In fact, JavaBeans are not thread-safe.

However, a JavaBean can effectively be thread-safe depending on its scope. Since both the `request` and `page` scopes have an instance-based lifespan, it is impossible to have threading problems with a JavaBean within these scopes.

On first glance, `session`-based JavaBeans seem to be thread-safe. In this case, the JavaBean is only available to one particular Session ID so it's not likely that a threading problem will arise, but it is still possible for threading problems to occur. In particular, if a user has two windows open from the same browser or the user clicks on a Submit button twice, this will create two separate requests that might wind up causing a race condition. So, in real-world situations, it is not useful to view `session` JavaBeans as thread-safe.

Of course, JavaBeans created in the `application` scope are simply not thread-safe. If a JavaBean should be used in this scope, then the developer will need to make sure that the Java-Bean is internally thread-safe.

It's generally a good idea to always try to make JavaBeans that are as thread-safe as possible. This allows the Java Bean developer and JSP authors to work without fear that the bean might be used in an unexpected scope. But sometimes, the nature of a JavaBean can make it difficult or impossible to make the JavaBean completely thread-safe.

◆ 9.3 Components and Component Frameworks

A component is a packaged set of code that communicates with other components through a set of methods called interfaces. Developers simply examine the interfaces of different components and connect them to form applications. Newer technology allows components to be created on different platforms with different programming languages, as well as allowing components on remote computers to be tied together to form a single application.

The software that ties components together to form an application is called a component framework. Component frameworks are a major part of enterprise programming today. There are three major component frameworks available today: Microsoft has created a component framework called the Component Object Model (COM), or Distributed Component Object Model (DCOM); the Open Software Foundation (OSF) has developed the Common Object Request Broker Architecture (CORBA); and the third component framework is Enterprise JavaBeans (EJB).

◆ 9.4 Enterprise JavaBeans

EJB are composed of server components written in Java that are distributed across a network. In the simplest sense, they are Java-Beans that can be distributed across a network using Java's distributed object model RMI (Remote Method Invocation).

EJB are much more complex than normal JavaBeans. They have a set of additional concepts and restrictions that help define them as EJB.

Since EJB are fairly complex, they typically require a special application server that knows how to handle the EJB container. Several of the more advanced JSP engines directly support EJB, but it's by no means a standard feature.

Because of the complexity of EJB and the additional require-ment of a specialized server, they are outside of the scope of this book. It is helpful to understand how EJB differ from normal JavaBeans and the advantages of one vs. the other.

9.4.1 Session Beans vs. Entity Beans

EJB basically come in two basic types: session beans and entity beans. A session bean represents a client to the application. The client communicates with the application server by invoking methods that belong to the EJB. A session bean can be thought of as an extension of the client. As far as the application server is concerned, it is the client. Each session bean can have only one client. When the client terminates, its corresponding session bean also terminates. Therefore, a session bean is transient, or non-persistent.

An entity bean represents an object in some persistent stor-age. This persistent storage could be a database, a file, or any other storage mechanism. An entity bean might represent a cus-tomer whose information is stored as a row in a relational data-base table. The persistence of an entity bean can either be managed by the EJB container or the entity bean itself. However, if the entity bean manages its own state, then it will need to in-clude code on how to access its data, which removes a significant layer of abstraction and could violate EJB rules.

9.4.2 Programming Restrictions for Enterprise Beans

EJB work by making use of the services provided by the EJB con-tainer in the application server. This container and application server are responsible for life-cycle management and interaction between beans.

To avoid conflicts with these services, enterprise beans are ex-plicitly restricted from performing operations involving manag-ing threads, using any file services in `java.io`, listening on sockets, or using native libraries.

Also, since EJB are typically used to represent business logic and processes, it's very common for EJB to have restrictions on the types of presentations they can make. For example, EJB are explicitly restricted from manipulating window components.

◆ 9.5 Recap

JavaBeans are a powerful programming addition to Java, and their use in JSP pages helps migrate Web programming to a component model. JavaBeans serve as the business logic layer, while JSP pages act as the presentation logic. In this way, more scalable and powerful Web applications can be built.

10 Using Custom Tags

IN THIS CHAPTER

- Custom Tag Basics
- The Custom Tag API
- Creating a New Custom Tag
- Recap

When it comes to design strategy, there have been two different themes in this book: first, try to write code in a component-based design; and second, try and separate presentation logic from business logic. One method of doing this is the JavaBean, which allows the JSP page to serve as a front end for presentation, while the JavaBean itself is used for business logic.

Other examples have made use of including JSP files using the include *action (*`<jsp:include ... />`*) and* include *directive (*`<%@ include ... %>`*). Each of these methods works in different ways, but both present significant problems for scalability and portability.*

In the end, the JSP specification authors realized that there needed to be a way to create custom JSP actions, or custom tags. Not only would this provide a portable way of defining and creating JSP libraries, but it would also provide an interface for JSP tools to share these libraries.

◆ 10.1 Custom Tag Basics

Tag libraries are extremely powerful, and thus fairly complex. They incorporate all of the tag features of JSP actions, such as supporting nested actions, scripting elements, and the creation of scripting variables. They can be used to instantiate objects, and are scripting language-neutral. Probably their most powerful feature is that the JSP author can develop a component and never need to understand the inner workings of the tag library, or even the calling methods.

While they are an advanced technique for the JSP author, they are a major step towards separation of business logic and presentation logic. Defined from the start to be portable, they are also an excellent mechanism for creating and distributing functions from JSP page to JSP page.

10.1.1 Custom Tag Syntax

The custom tag syntax is exactly the same as the syntax of JSP actions. The JSP action prefix is `jsp`, while a custom tag prefix is determined by the `prefix` attribute of the `taglib` directive used to instantiate a set of custom tags. The prefix is followed by a colon and the name of the tag itself.

The actions tag does not have separate JSP and XML formats because it already is in the XML format. It is the same with custom tags. The colon-delimited tag name is actually part of the XML namespaces standard. The format of a standard custom tag looks like the following:

```
<utility:repeat number="12">Hello World!</utility:repeat>
```

Here, a tag library named `utility` is referenced. The specific tag used is named `repeat`. The tag has an attribute named `number`, which is assigned a value of `"12"`. The tag contains a body that has the text `"Hello World!"`, and then the tag is closed.

Besides being able to define its own attributes, custom tags can have an `id` attribute, which allows the tag to create new objects and assign them a scripting variable.

```
<htmltool:table id="tabletag" border="0" />
<% tabletag.setCols(5); %>
```

In the above example, the `tag` table is used from the `htmltool` tag library. The `id` attribute creates a scripting element called `tabletag`, which refers to the new object created by this custom tag. In the following line, this new scripting element is used to call the `setCols()` method of the custom tag instance.

Hopefully these examples show that custom tags have an almost identical structure to JSP action tags. They should also show the complex number of variations that custom tags can have. This becomes important when programming new custom tags, as they will have to possibly account for attributes, body data, and new scripting elements within their classes.

10.1.2 The Players

Tag extensions are very complex. Beyond the custom tags themselves, there are actually several different components that are all necessary for custom tags to work. First there is the tag library, which are the classes that make up the Java program called by the custom tags. Next is the `taglib` directive, which is used to identify the tag library as well as associate it with a tag namespace prefix. Finally, there is the tag library descriptor (TLD). This is an XML document that describes the tag library. Each of these components must be in place before custom tags can be used.

THE TAG LIBRARY AND TAG HANDLERS

The tag library is a collection of actions that add functionality to a JSP page. They are classes that provide the functionality of the custom tag. While tag libraries can be distributed several ways, it is common for them to be contained in a JAR file. When distributed in a JAR file, the TLD must be included in the META-INF directory and named `taglib.tld`.

Tag libraries can also be distributed in a special format called a Web application archive (WAR) file. Creating and using WAR files are discussed in the next chapter.

Tag libraries are tied to the `taglib` directive by the `uri` attribute of the `taglib` directive. It can be any valid URI as long as it can be used to identify the semantics of the tag library.

At the heart of the tag library is the tag handler. The tag handler is a server-side object that is created to evaluate actions during the execution of a JSP page. Every tag library extends one of the tag handler classes. It supports a protocol that handles the passing of information between the JSP page and the custom tag.

Tag handlers are simply JavaBeans. There are two interfaces to tag handlers: `Tag` and `BodyTag`. `Tag` is used for simple constructs that are not interested in manipulating the body content of the custom tag. `BodyTag` is an extension of `Tag` and gives the tag handler access to what is between the open and close tags. Two classes, `TagSupport` and `TagBodySupport`, can be used as base classes when creating new tag handlers.

THE `taglib` DIRECTIVE

The `taglib` directive is the mechanism that ties the TLD to the JSP page, as well as sets the tag namespace prefix to be used in the JSP page. It has two attributes, both of which are required.

The `uri` attribute contains a Universal Resource Identifier (URI) that points to the location of the tag library. In the case of a JAR file distribution of a tag library, the URI points to the JAR file itself, which contains the TLD in the form of a `taglib.tld` file.

The `prefix` attribute identifies the XML namespace prefix that will identify tags that are part of the new tag library. The namespaces available to a JSP page are limited to the default `jsp` namespace as well as any namespace created by the `taglib` directive. An example `taglib` directive might look like:

```
<%@ taglib

uri="http://www.javadesktop.com/taglib/htmltool.jar" prefix="tool"
    %>
```

The `uri` attribute here tells the JSP engine that the tag specified is located in the file at: `http://www.javadesktop.com/taglib/htmltool.jar`. The `prefix` attribute tells the JSP engine that all tags beginning with `<tool:tagname>` should be routed to the tag handler associated with `htmltool.jar`.

THE TAG LIBRARY DESCRIPTOR

The TLD is an XML document that describes a tag library. It is used by the JSP container to interpret pages that contain `taglib` directives. It can also be used by JSP authoring tools that generate JSP pages using tag libraries.

The TLD is basically a set of metadata about a tag library. It describes the tag library as a whole, as well as describing its individual tags, attributes, version numbers, and other information. Each action in the tag library is listed in the TLD. Information contained for each action includes its name, the class that contains its tag handler, and all of its attributes.

The distinct advantage of having a TLD file is that tools can find out information about a tag library without having to instantiate objects or load libraries. This is a standard approach that is used in many parts of the Java 2 Enterprise Edition (J2EE).

TLD documents, as they are XML, follow an XML DTD (document type definition). The official DTD is described at *http://java.sun.com/j2ee/dtds/web-jstaglibrary_1_1.dtd* for JSP specification 1.1 and at *http://java.sun.com/dtd/web-jsptaglibrary_1_2.dtd* for JSP specification 1.2.

CUSTOM TAG TYPES

There are many different types of custom tags. Some tags interpret the tag body, while others do not. Some tags instantiate new objects, while many do not. Each of these custom tag types has to be approached differently from the custom tag programmer's perspective. Table 10-1 takes a look at the different types of custom tags as well as the differences between them.

TABLE 10-1 Different Actions

No Body or Objects

```
<mytag:tag myattr="foo" />
```

The simplest type of custom tag has no body and creates no new objects. Without processing the body, the custom tag would extend the TagSupport class.

A Body with No Objects

```
<mytag:tag myattr="foo">Hello!</mytag:tag>
```

A custom tag that evaluates the body of its tag but does not create any objects is more difficult. Instead of extending TagSupport, it extends TagBodySupport. A processing loop is created to iterate through the body of the tag until all processing is complete. This can be especially complicated when the tag body contains subtags.

No Body with New Objects

```
<mytag:tag myattr="foo" id="mytag"/>
```

Again, without processing the body, the custom tag would extend the TagSupport class. In this case, a new object is created and assigned to a scripting element called "mytag". Having a new object that relates to a scripting element is somewhat of a complicated task. The key is to synchronize the value of the new scripting element with the object. This is done through the TagExtraInfo class. Each time a new object and scripting element is created this class must be created. The information that the TagExtraInfo class contains is all of the names and types of the scripting elements that will be assigned objects. It is the custom tag author's responsibility to make sure this class is created and has the right information.

A Body with New Objects

```
<mytag:tag id="mytag"/>Hello!</mytag:tag>
```

This is the most difficult type of custom tag, as both the complexity of extending the `TagBodySupport` class as well as the creation of a `TagExtraInfo` class is necessary. This type of custom tag implements all of the possible specifications of a custom tag, including attributes, evaluating the body, and creating new objects and scripting elements.

It is also important to note that a custom tag can have any number of parameters, and can even have no parameters at all. This also plays a significant role in the programming complexity of a custom tag.

◆ 10.2 The Custom Tag API

Before reviewing an example custom tag, it is a good idea to take a look at the interfaces and methods used by tag libraries.

10.2.1 Special Methods and Constants for Custom Tags

The tables below are listed from the assumption that tags will be created to extend `BodyTagSupport`. Information on the methods for other extensions can be found in the API reference at *http://java.sun.com/*.

One of the most significant features that custom tags have is their ability to change the behavior of the page. This is done by simply changing the value that the tag returns.

Every custom tag should return a known value, or a predefined constant. Table 10–2 shows the static return constants that dictate how the JSP page should process.

TABLE 10–2 Static Constants

```
static int SKIP_BODY
```

Skip body evaluation.

```
static int EVAL_BODY_TAG
```

Request the creation of new `bodyContent` on which to evaluate the body of this tag.

```
static int EVAL_BODY_INCLUDE
```

Evaluate body into existing output stream.

```
static int EVAL_PAGE
```

Continue evaluating the page.

```
static int SKIP_PAGE
```

Skip the rest of the page.

A method summary is provided in Table 10–3.

TABLE 10–3 Method Signatures

```
int doEndTag()
```

Process the end tag. This method will be called on all tag objects. All instance states associated with this instance must be reset.

```
int doStartTag()
```

Process the start tag for this instance. The `doStartTag()` method assumes that all setter methods have already been invoked and that the body has not yet been invoked.

```
static Tag findAncestorWithClass(Tag from, java.lang.Class classnm)
```

Find the nearest instance of a given class type that is closest to a given instance. This class is used for coordination among cooperating tags.

```
java.lang.String getId()
```

The value of the `id` attribute of this tag or null.

```
Tag getParent()
```

The `Tag` instance enclosing this `Tag` instance.

```
java.lang.Object getValue(java.lang.String name)
```

Get a value.

```
java.util.Enumeration getValues()
```

Enumerate the values.

```
void release()
```

`release()` called after `doEndTag()` to reset state.

```
void removeValue(java.lang.String name)
```

Remove a value.

```
void setId(java.lang.String id)
```

Set the `id` attribute.

void setPageContext(PageContext pageContext)

Set the page context.

void setParent(Tag someTag)

Set the nesting tag of this tag.

void setValue(java.lang.String name, java.lang.Object value)

Set a value.

JspWriter getPreviousOut()

Get surrounding out.

int doAfterBody()

Actions after some body has been evaluated. Not invoked in empty tags or in tags returning SKIP_BODY in doStartTag(). This method is invoked after every body evaluation. The pair "BODY" and "doAfterBody()" is invoked initially if doStartTag() returned EVAL_BODY_TAG, and it is repeated as long as the doAfterBody() evaluation returns EVAL_BODY_TAG. The method re-invocations may lead to different actions because there might have been some changes to shared state, or because of external computation.

void doInitBody()

Prepare for evaluation of the body. It will be invoked at most once per action invocation. Will not be invoked if there is no body evaluation. Frequently, it is not redefined by the tag author.

BodyContent getBodyContent()

Get current bodyContent.

void setBodyContent(BodyContent someBody)

Prepare for evaluation of the body. It will be invoked at most once per action invocation. Will not be invoked if there is no body evaluation. Frequently, it is redefined by the tag author.

10.2.2 Understanding the Tag Library Descriptor File

The TLD file is used to describe everything about a tag library. In fact, everything the JSP page knows about the tag is acquired from this file.

The JSP engine actually builds the method signatures that are available by reading this file. Minor errors in this file can cause some interesting errors in a state that the constructor's signature does not match the method call.

TABLE 10–4 Tag Library Descriptor Entities

`taglib`	Parent class.
`tlibversion`	Version of `taglib` that should be used.
`jspversion`	Version of JSP that should be used.
`shortname`	Handle for the tag library—this is the first part of the tag name on a JSP page.
`uri`	A unique identifier—this doesn't actually have to point anywhere; in fact, it doesn't need to be a URI, but it's still good practice to really have it be a URI to the library.
`info`	Description for the tag library.
`tag`	Tag definition (contains subsets: `name`, `tagclass`, `body-Content`, `info`, and `attribute`)
Tag Subsets	
`name`	Name of tag. This is the second part of the tag name on a JSP page.
`tagclass`	Name of class.
`bodyContent`	Type of content ("Empty", "JSP", or "tag-dependent").
`info`	Description of tag.
`attribute`	Tag attributes (contains subsets: `name`, `required`, and `rtexpvalue`)
Attribute Subsets	
`name`	Name of attribute.
`required`	Required (`true`/`false`).
`rtexprvalue`	Value translated by JSP (true/false).

The TLD file follows an XML style of syntax, so it includes nested structures. Fortunately, it's a fairly simple file and is relatively easy to break down into logical blocks (see Table 10–4).

10.2.3 Special Packaging Considerations

When a new tag library is created it needs to be packaged in a JAR file with the TLD. The TLD needs to be put into the META-INF directory so that the JAR file will be used as a tag library.

The `jar` command does not provide command-line switches to include non-manifest files in the META-INF directory, so this needs to be done by brute force. A META-INF directory needs to be created in parallel with the source tree. Then, when the JAR is created the META-INF directory needs to be explicitly added. For example:

```
jar cf taglib.jar com/javadesktop/taglib/* META-INF/*
```

◆ 10.3 Creating a New Custom Tag

Script 10.1 shows an example of using custom tags. The example creates a new tag that iterates through a section of the JSP page a certain number of times. The functional components will be discussed after each component has been presented.

Script 10.1
LoopTag.jsp

```
package com.javadesktop.utiltags;

import javax.servlet.jsp.*;
import javax.servlet.jsp.tagext.*;

public class LoopTag extends BodyTagSupport {
  private int maxCount = 0;
  private int currentCount = 0;

  public void setCount(int count) {
    this.maxCount = count;
  }

  public int doStartTag() {
    if (currentCount < maxCount) {
      return EVAL_BODY_TAG;
    } else {
      return SKIP_BODY;
    }
  }

  public int doAfterBody() throws JspException {
    currentCount++;

    if (currentCount < maxCount) {
      return EVAL_BODY_TAG;
    } else {
      return SKIP_BODY;
    }
  }

  public int doEndTag() throws JspException {
```

```
    try {
      if(bodyContent != null)
          bodyContent.writeOut(bodyContent.getEnclosing-
Writer());
      } catch(java.io.IOException e) {
    throw new JspException("IO Error: " + e.getMessage());
      }

      return EVAL_PAGE;
    }

  public void release() {
    super.release();
    currentCount = 0;
    }
}
```

Script 10.1 is the meat and bones of this custom tag. It does all the work in managing the iterations, handling whether the data should be displayed or not.

The class signature and first method are not really remarkable. They resemble a JavaBean, except the class extends `Body-TagSupport`. The more interesting sections are the other methods in the file.

The `doStartTag()` method will be run when the tag is first called. It checks if there are iterations to do. If there are no iterations to do, then the `SKIP_BODY` constant is returned, which says essentially, "Ignore everything between the start and end tags." If there are iterations to be done, the `EVAL_BODY_TAG` is returned that says, "Process everything between the start and end tags."

Next in the source code is the `doAfterBody()` method. Each time the body is processed, this method is called. This method first increments the iteration counter. Next, it does the same thing the `doStartTag()` method did—if there is more iteration, process the body. Since this method is called after each body is processed, it creates the loop.

Next, the `doEndTag()` occurs. This is called when closing the tags. This tag contains a particularly interesting-looking piece of code:

```
  try {
    if(bodyContent != null)

  bodyContent.writeOut(bodyContent.getEnclosingWriter());
    } catch(java.io.IOException e) {
      throw new JspException("IO Error: " + e.getMessage());
  }
```

All this code is doing is printing the content of the body. Unfortunately, this needs to done in this manner because the custom tag does not have access to the out object of the JSP page. The writer needs to be found indirectly, using getEnclosing-Writer(); then, it is pushed to the JspWriter using writeOut().

Finally, there is the release() method that is called when the processing tag is done and needs to clean up. It simply uses the superclass provided by the tag interface and resets the counter.

10.3.1 The Tag Library Descriptor

To actually create a custom tag, there needs to be a TLD, taglib.tld. Script 10.2 shows the TLD for the first example of custom tags.

Script 10.2
taglib.tld

```
<?xml version="1.0" encoding="ISO-8859-1" ?>
<!DOCTYPE taglib PUBLIC
"-//Sun Microsystems, Inc.//DTD JSP Tag Library 1.1//EN"
"http://java.sun.com/products/jsp/dtd/web-
     jsptaglib_1_1.dtd">

<taglib>
  <tlibversion>1.0</tlibversion>
  <jspversion>1.1</jspversion>
  <shortname>util</shortname>
  <uri>http://www.javadesktop.com/taglib/utiltags.jar
  </uri>
  <info>Util Tag library</info>
  <tag>
    <name>loop</name>

  <tagclass>com.javadesktop.utiltags.LoopTag</tagclass>
    <bodycontent>JSP</bodycontent>
    <info>Allows looping</info>
    <attribute>
      <name>count</name>
      <required>true</required>
      <rtexprvalue>false</rtexprvalue>
    </attribute>
  </tag>
</taglib>
```

The TLD file has a major effect on how the tags will be exposed to the JSP page. By examining this file, it should be fairly easy to figure out the tags that will be made available by this new tag library.

In particular, the `<shortname>` tag identifies the name of the library, `'util'`. The `<name>` tag identifies the methods that will be made available; in this case, there is only one, `'loop'`. Finally, the `<attribute>` tag identifies the arguments for each tag; again in this case, only one is available, `'count'`. So, the actual tag that will be used from this library will look like this on the JSP page:

```
<util:loop count="n">
```

10.3.2 Custom Tags in Action

The new library needs to be packaged up as a file with the TLD and put into the CLASSPATH. Now this new tag can be accessed from any JSP page on the server. Script 10.3 shows a JSP page that uses this new tag library.

Script 10.3
looptest.jsp

```
<%@ taglib
    uri="http://www.javadesktop.com/taglib/utiltags.jar"
      prefix="util"
%>

<html>
<head><title>Stitch Magazine! Loop Test</title></head>
<body>

<table border=0 cellpadding=3 cellspacing=5>
<util:loop count="5">
  <tr>
  <util:loop count="5">
    <td bgcolor=#ccccff align=center>
    <b><%= (int)(Math.random()*9)+1 %></b>
    </td>
  </util:loop>
  </tr>
</util:loop>
</table>

</body>
</html>
```

While the looping feature is very powerful, this specific example is fairly trivial. It generates a grid of random numbers. It's

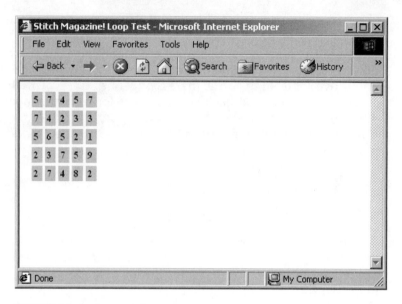

FIGURE 10–1 Output of `looptest.jsp`

not very complex, but it does show how the tag would be used and even shows that the tag is easily nested.

Figure 10–1 shows the output from `looptest.jsp`.

◆ 10.4 Recap

Custom tags are some of the most promising features of JSP. They allow better separation of Java code and HTML presentation, as well as a standard, portable way to distribute software libraries. Custom tags allow JSP authors the ability to implement a component without knowledge of the internal layout or method signatures. They rely on a standard XML format for implementation, and are extremely similar to the JSP action tags.

More importantly, custom tags bring the JSP paradigm closer to the component model. Many Java code purists believe that mixing Java code and HTML code in the same file is a bad model. With custom tags, there is a complete separation of HTML presentation logic and Java business logic. While coding with custom tags is more complex, it has distinct advantages in scalability, portability, and component design. As JSP continues to evolve, look for the role of custom tags to expand.

Chapter 11 Deploying JSP Applications

In This Chapter

- Reducing Complexity with Decomposition
- JSP Application Deployment
- Recap

In addition to the need to develop a JSP program is the need to architect a JSP application to suit the production needs of a project. These needs generally fall into two areas: architecture design and program deployment.

Design involves creating a central strategy around which the application is to be developed. This involves many things, including program workflow, message flow, and shared access to outside data sources. Designing an architecture for an application is similar to laying the foundation of a building. It is the framework on which the entire application must rely. The enterprise application needs of scalability, availability, upgrade-ability, and management all rely on a solid application framework. Is the application composed in such a way that a large development team can work simultaneously? Do minor functionality changes demand a major application change, or simply re-coding one component? These questions should be answered by designing the right architecture before application development begins.

Application deployment plays an equally important role in the life cycle of software development. By what means is the application to be distributed or released into production? What is the process for moving an application to a testing environment? What is the process for upgrading or patching an application already in production? These deci-

sions should be made during the application design phase to accommo-date the development and testing phases of the software development life cycle.

◆ 11.1 Reducing Complexity with Decomposition

The most effective way of designing an application architecture is by decomposing an application into separate components. This is the underlying theme in all modern forms of design and is the foundation of object-oriented development. Component-based architectures are built on the concept of modules, which can be developed, changed, or upgraded independently of the entire application. This builds a high level of abstraction, and allows applications to be developed in team environments. It also produces code that is more maintainable than applications with a centralized design.

However, application architects should be wary of the amount of granularity used with component-based design. While decomposing an application into separate components has many benefits, separating components into too granular a framework can actually make an application more complex. The key is to have a sound organization to the separation of components, and to size the level of component granularity with the size of both the application and the development team.

11.1.1 Methods for Architecting JSP Components

There are several methods that can be used to physically separate JSP applications into different components. Each of these has advantages and disadvantages based on the type of application, the size of the application, and the skill level of the application developers.

The first method is the most simple. It involves creating different components in different JSP pages and combining them with dynamic `include` actions. The second method is by far the most prevalent, and involves connecting a JSP page to external JavaBeans or EJBs. The third method is rapidly growing in popularity, and involves creating modules in tag libraries.

Each of these different methods has different strengths and weaknesses based on individual situations, and in general it is best to combine these methods and utilize them where they have the most advantages.

USING DYNAMIC PAGE INCLUDES

By utilizing `include` action tags, individual JSP page components can be created as separate JSP files. This is very similar to using dynamic Server-Side Includes (SSIs). While this can be a quick and dirty way of creating reusable code, the inherent problems of this architecture are significant.

There are scalability issues with this method. Another issue is the difficulty involved in sharing information between the pages. Further, there is no standardized interface for connecting the components (JSP pages) together. There is also the inability of one JSP author to work with another's code without large amounts of documentation, detailed comments, and an understanding of general strategy.

Despite all of these drawbacks, using `include` actions does serve a good purpose and they are perfect for many different types of situations. This is especially true with small applications or small components that only provide limited functionality. Used in combination with other component methods, they help compose a good component programming "arsenal."

USING JAVABEANS AND ENTERPRISE JAVABEANS

In the world of Java programming, JavaBeans are considered the de-facto standard for component programming. They have come a long way from their original intended use as GUI components. Most Java servlet and JSP authors consider them to be the standard method of creating Java components. However, due to their ability to be used in many different situations, there are a few inherent features of JavaBeans that are not perfectly suited for JSP page authoring. In general these disadvantages are seen as a limitation of connecting JSP page and JavaBeans technologies together, and not limitations of the JavaBeans API itself.

ADVANTAGES AND DISADVANTAGES OF USING JAVABEANS WITH JSP

Some of the disadvantages of using JavaBeans with JSP are inherent in the functionality and design of JavaBeans, but they affect JSP programming nonetheless. The advantages all lean toward the benefits of object-oriented programming, with emphasis on code reusability and maintainability, as well as component design.

Probably the most common complaint about JavaBeans is the required use of a standard, argument-less constructor. In cases where a single attribute needs to be sent to a JavaBean, it is cumbersome to use both the `useBean` and `setProperty` tags.

In addition the JSP JavaBean syntax is often seen as very cumbersome. For example:

```
<jsp:useBean id="myBean" class="MyBean" scope="session">
<jsp:setProperty name="myBean" property="prop"
            value="val">
```

can easily be replaced with:

```
<%
    MyBean myBean
       = (MyBean)session.getAttribute("myBean");
    if (myBean == null) {
      myBean = new MyBean();
      session.setAttribute("myBean", myBean);
    }
    myBean.setProp("val");
%>
```

While the former takes up less space, it is argued that the latter is more readable to the average Java programmer. It also gives better insight to what actions are actually being performed.

Another common criticism of using JavaBeans with JSP is the awkwardness of the getProperty and setProperty tags. It is cumbersome to set JavaBean properties that are not strings. There is String conversion for the basic types such as int, byte, or char. In addition, request parameters can be used to set properties. If the JSP author needs to set a property of another type, the only method using the setProperty tag is to use a request-time computation, such as an expression. This begs the question: Why use an expression within a setProperty tag when the property can be set directly within a scriptlet? None of the methods for using a setProperty tag with a non-string value are straightforward.

Furthermore, getting objects with the getProperty tag forces the data to be formatted within the standard toString() method of the object. This is useless in situations where the results of the toString() method don't contain usable data. For example, most of the collections classes, such as Vector or HashMap, tend to use toString() as a debugging tool. In addition, the JSP JavaBean action tags do not support indexed (multi-value) properties within JavaBeans. This means that there is no straightforward way to send multiple-value objects to and from JavaBeans using JSP JavaBean actions.

While there are many difficulties with utilizing JavaBeans in JSP pages, they are still seen as a superior architecture due to their component programming benefits. JavaBeans minimize the amount of code in JSP. This is a definite step forward toward a separation of presentation and application logic. It is generally accepted that it is much easier to maintain a Web application if you keep the JSP code to a minimum.

JavaBeans also support introspection, which allows an IDE (integrated developer environment) to provide a visual design feature. When moving in "Internet time," there is enormous value in integrating components into IDEs for rapid application development.

Additionally, JavaBeans promote a more reusable, object-oriented design. By using JavaBeans, other Java applications, such as applets or standalone applications, can utilize their functionality.

Finally, and probably most importantly, the JavaBeans API is simple. JavaBeans can be used to make small, lightweight components that are easy to implement and use. JSP developers can learn the basic concepts of JavaBeans very quickly and begin writing and using simple components with very little effort.

USING TAG LIBRARIES WITH JSP

Using tag libraries is covered heavily in the previous chapter. Tag libraries are a relatively new technology. In general, developing tag libraries is seen as a large amount of work, but using the custom tags that are created is seen as a straightforward task. Page designers with limited Java skills, as well as visual development environments, should be able to use tag libraries easily.

THE ADVANTAGES AND DISADVANTAGES OF USING TAG LIBRARIES

By far the biggest disadvantage of using tag libraries is their complexity. Several different components must come together for custom tags to work. Besides the tags themselves, there are the `taglib` directive, the tag library, and the TLD. Each of these components must be written correctly and stored in specific locations for tag libraries to work.

Due to the complex nature of tag libraries, they are also hard to set up and deploy. Additionally, limited support for tag libraries existed at the time this book was written, making the use of tag libraries dependent on the application platform selected.

Another limitation of tag libraries is their suitability for components outside of JSP. While a JavaBean can be created that serves as a back-end for both a standalone application as well as a JSP page, tag libraries are specifically limited to JSP programming.

There are several advantages to using tag libraries. First and foremost is that they are simple to use. The JSP author does not need to understand the inner workings of a custom tag to be able to develop with it. Custom tags are used in the exact same way as JSP action tags, making them scripting language-neutral.

Tag libraries can also be extremely useful with visual development environments. It's likely that many standard HTML editors will support the use of custom tags in the near future. Because they are portable in nature and use XML as a configuration language, they are perfect for integrating into IDEs.

Tag libraries are an excellent way to separate Java code from the presentation layer. They are the perfect solution for creating templates or for including control-flow operations into JSP pages in a component-based, reusable manner.

Tag libraries, just like JavaBeans and `include` actions, have their own advantages and disadvantages. Taken together, these three methods allow you many different ways to decompose JSP pages into reusable components.

11.1.2 JSP Design Models

Having taken a look at the different physical levels that JSP applications can be broken down into, it is important to have an overall strategy or organization for how the different components relate.

Most JSP applications fall into two levels of component organization, separated by the role or responsibility each component plays in the application life cycle. The first level of separation is natural in JSP applications, as it was the foundation on which JSP was developed. This is the separation of presentation logic from application logic. Often called page-centric design, this model can be thought of as a typical "JSP-only" application. In early JSP specifications, this model was called Model 1 (see Figure 11-1).

A second level of component organization is to take the existing Model 1 and separate the controller logic from the presentation logic. This model is called Model 2, and is often referred to as a servlet-oriented design, due to the fact that it is almost always implemented with both JSP pages and Java servlets. Model 2 has separate components to deal with the user interface, application, and user interaction (see Figure 11-2).

To further understand these concepts, it is a good idea to get a solid understanding of the differences between presentation, application, and controller logic.

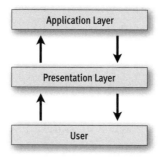

FIGURE 11-1 Separation of Application and Presentation Logic

PRESENTATION LOGIC

Presentation logic is the part of the application that deals with the presentation layer. It deals with the user interface and Web-based elements such as HTML and XML. Presentation logic is concerned with displaying the information, not how the information was retrieved or how the application chose to display the information.

Presentation logic components can also contain logic about the direction the application will flow based on user input. When this happens there is no controller component. In other words, it handles not just displaying information to the user, but receiving information as well. In the case of JSP, this means handling both the HTTP request as well as the response. When presentation logic contains logic to process the HTTP request, there is no separation of presentation logic from controller logic.

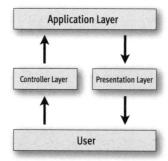

FIGURE 11-2 Separation of Presentation and Controller Logic

CONTROLLER LOGIC

Controller logic may or may not be present in the presentation logic, and this is the delineation between the different levels of JSP application component separation. Controller logic "controls" the application flow and serves as the connector between the user interface and the application.

In the JSP application, the controller logic receives and interprets the HTTP request, deciding the next step of the application based on user input. When there is a separation of controller logic, the presentation layer simply concerns itself with the HTTP response.

A key function of the controller layer is the management of connections to the application layer. In the case of JavaBeans, this means instantiating and connecting to the JavaBeans, as well as passing the results to the presentation layer.

APPLICATION LOGIC

Application logic is the center of the application. The application logic is responsible for the logic behind what the application is supposed to accomplish. For example, in a Web-based registration system, the application logic would consist of taking the submitted name, checking it against the database, adding it to the database, and returning a result.

It is important to point out that there is no user interface logic in the application layer. This means that the application logic components can reside completely outside the JSP application, in an EJB or CORBA API for example.

One of the great benefits of a separate application logic layer is the ability to have multiple user interfaces to the same application. A Swing Java standalone application can connect to the same JavaBeans that a JSP application connects to and perform the same functionality through a different GUI.

MODEL 1: SEPARATING PRESENTATION AND APPLICATION LOGIC

JSP Model 1 is what is thought of as the traditional JSP architecture (See Figure 11–3). In Model 1, the browser sends a request to the JSP page. The JSP page connects to JavaBeans to process the application logic and connect to data sources. The JSP page then connects to the JavaBean and sends a response to the browser. There is a separation of presentation and application logic.

JSP Model 1 is seen as a reasonable solution for fairly simple applications. Issues arise when the logic contained within the JSP

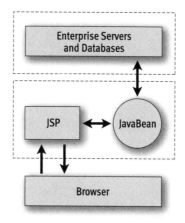

FIGURE 11–3 Model 1 JSP
Architecture

page grows. With a large amount of logic, there tends to be a lot
of scriptlets or Java code within the JSP page. This is often the case
with large applications. As a Java developer, this may not seem a
problem, but when designers maintain the JSP page, an issue can
arise from having large amounts of Java code on a JSP page.

In essence, the problem is that having two roles, application
logic and presentation logic, is no longer sufficient to have a
good separation of code. As more and more logic surrounds processing the HTTP request, there is a greater need for separate
"controller" logic to guide the flow of data and logic within the
application. This idea gives birth to JSP Model 2.

MODEL 2: SEPARATING CONTROLLER
AND PRESENTATION LOGIC

JSP Model 2 adds a Java servlet to the architecture to fulfill the
role of processing the HTTP request and controlling data and
logic flow. It decides what JSP page to forward based on the
request. It is also responsible for instantiating or connecting to
any JavaBeans for application logic. (See Figure 11–4)

This model takes advantage of the strengths of both servlets
and JSP pages. Servlets are especially strong in processing-
intensive tasks, and JSP pages are excellent for presenting data.

The three roles that make up the JSP Model 2 often mimic the
roles of enterprise development projects. There is often a team for
a core programming API represented by the JavaBeans or EJB.
Another team might represent creating a Web-based front-end
for the API, much as another team might develop a Java Swing-

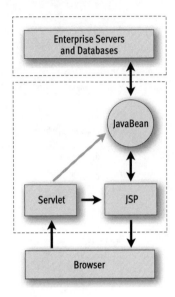

FIGURE 11–4 Model 2 JSP Architecture

based front-end. This is represented by the servlet or controller logic. Finally, the JSP pages represent the designers or creative team of the development project. All in all, the Model 2 design pattern adds a new layer of abstraction to the JSP application development process, helping to scale the development of large enterprise applications.

Script 11.1 shows a simple controller servlet that determines which of three JSP pages to forward based on user input. It first handles new clients that do not have sessions by forwarding them to the login JSP page. Next, the servlet determines the value of the request attribute "action". If action is equal to "EDIT", the page is forwarded to editData.jsp, otherwise the page is forwarded to viewData.jsp. Note that there are no JavaBeans instantiated inside of ControllerServlet.java as it is not necessary in this example. This is often the case in more complicated applications where more processing is needed to determine the appropriate course of action. ControllerServlet.java is a basic example of how controller logic is separated from presentation logic in JSP Model 2.

It is important to note that the ideas behind Model 2 are not new. They are based on a tried and tested programming pattern that predates Java itself. In fact, JSP Model 2 mirrors the ideas behind the Model-View-Controller (MVC) architecture developed for the SmallTalk programming environment.

Script 11.1
ControllerServlet.java

```java
import java.util.*;
import java.io.*;
import javax.servlet.*;
import javax.servlet.http.*;

public class ControllerServlet extends HttpServlet {

  public void doPost
      (HttpServletRequest req, HttpServletResponse res)
      throws ServletException, IOException {

    HttpSession session = req.getSession(false);
    if (session == null) {
      res.sendRedirect("/jsp/login.jsp");
    }

    ServletContext sc = getServletContext();
    String action = req.getParameter("action");

    if (!action.equals("EDIT")) {
      String url="/jsp/editData.jsp";
    } else {
      String url="/jsp/viewData.jsp";
    }

    RequestDispatcher rd = sc.getRequestDispatcher(url);
    rd.forward(req, res);

  }

  public void doGet
      (HttpServletRequest req, HttpServletResponse res)
      throws ServletException, IOException {
    doPost(req, res);
  }
}
```

Remember that both Model 1 and Model 2 are viable JSP application strategies. Only by carefully analyzing the size and scope of an application, the development environment, and the skill set of the development team can the right model be chosen for a particular application.

11.2 JSP Application Deployment

Even before an application is created, a deployment strategy should be developed for the incremental, test, quality control, and production releases of the application. This strategy should take into account the installation and configuration of files not only in the first installation, but with successive upgrades as well. A well-planned deployment strategy saves time during the software development life cycle.

There are two basic methods for deploying an application. The first method is to deploy the application by a custom method. This means creating an install script that correctly deploys the application files in the proper location and configures them appropriately. While this is a non-standard method, it might be necessary for some complex or proprietary applications.

The second method is to use archive files. With archive files, such as JAR, WAR, and EAR files, there is a standard location as well as configuration for a Web application, including all of its associated files. Created and maintained correctly, archives can be deployed across multiple standard application servers with ease.

11.2.1 ZIP, JAR, WAR, and EAR

Early on in the development of Java, a need arose to package together files that compose Java applications. To resolve this problem, a series of different archive architectures has been developed to package files together into maintainable collections.

In the early stages, this collection of files was maintained in a ZIP (.zip) file. By using Phillip Katz's standard data compression format a series of Java classes could be packaged into a single file. Individual files could be read from this archive on an as-needed basis. But soon, the Java framers realized that there was a fair amount of metadata that was required in packaging Java files together for deployment. This gave birth to the Java archive, or JAR (.jar) file.

Java archives are still a collection of files compressed into a single file, but in addition, they contain specific information about how to deploy the files within the archive. This is most often implemented by creating a top-level directory in the archive titled META-INF. Inside the META-INF directory is a file called manifest.mf, which contains configuration information about the application, usually in colon-delimited name/value pairs. In Chapter 9, "Using JavaBeans," a manifest.mf file entry of `Java-Bean: true` was necessary to let the application server know that the Java classes were to be considered a JavaBean. While JAR files are still the most common type of archive used for distributing Java applications, the `manifest.mf` file has many limitations. It is a proprietary format, and the colon-delimited name/value pair is limited in its ability to describe complex configurations. With complex Web application architectures the `manifest.mf` file simply would not suffice. This led to the development of the Web archive, or WAR (`.war`) file.

WAR files were introduced with the Java Servlet API, but due to the close relationship of servlets and JSP pages, they serve as an excellent method for distributing JSP applications. WAR files are JAR files with a `.war` extension, so they maintain the same file compression of previous archives. A WAR file can contain more than just Java class files. Some example files include Java servlets, utility class files, JSP pages, static HTML and XML documents, JavaBeans, applets, and meta-information that ties the application together. The WAR file takes the idea of the `META-INF` directory and expands on its functionality. In a WAR file, there is a top-level directory called `WEB-INF`. This directory holds classes and files within its directory tree. An important file to note is `web.xml`, which is commonly known as the deployment descriptor. This file expands on the `manifest.mf` file by providing an XML format for standard, extensible configurations.

But alas, once again the WAR format was great for its use in deploying Web-centric Java servlet and JSP page applications, but it did not scale to extremely large enterprise applications that extended outside of the Web platform. To resolve this issue, a new Java archive format was created, called enterprise archives, or EAR (`.ear`) files.

Enterprise archives are a product of the Java 2 Enterprise Edition (J2EE). J2EE is a release of the Java development kit (JDK) that contains the APIs for creating enterprise applications. EAR files are seen as a super container for collecting multiple WAR and JAR files into a single application that is simple to deploy. For example, an application could have an HTML page to submit the user data, a servlet to process the data, and a JavaBean to store data in a database. The HTML page and servlet are stored in a WAR file, the JavaBean is stored in a JAR file, and the WAR and JAR files are both stored in an EAR file, which is deployed to production.

Configurations of EAR files and their related WAR and JAR files can be complicated, so bundled with the J2EE SDK (software development kit) is the Application Deployment Tool (DeployTool). This is a configuration tool for creating and editing JAR, WAR, and EAR files. Another powerful feature of DeployTool is its ability to connect directly to application servers to deploy EAR applications. DeployTool is a pure Java application that should run on any platform that supports J2EE.

11.2.2 Support for WAR and EAR Files

It should be noted that both WAR and EAR files were relatively new technologies at the time this book was written. Care should be taken to ensure that the application server or JSP engine selected for production supports WAR or EAR files before selecting them for a deployment strategy.

WAR FILES 101

WAR files are the archive of choice for deploying JSP applications. Within the WAR files, there is a directory structure that mimics the directory structure of a document root within a Web server. In addition, there is a WEB-INF directory that contains information about the configuration of the application, as well as classes and JAR files containing servlets, JavaBeans, and utility class files needed by the application.

The WEB-INF directory contains the web.xml file as well as two different directories: classes and lib. classes contain servlet and utility classes needed by the application. lib contains JAR files that might contain servlets, JavaBeans, and utility classes that might be useful to the application. Script 11.2 gives an example of a WAR file that might be the output of a jar tvf sample.war command. Note that the real difference between the lib and classes directory is whether or not the included Java classes are maintained in a JAR or are simply in their package hierarchy.

Script 11.2
A Sample WAR File

```
/index.html
/viewData.jsp
/editData.jsp
/images/logo.gif
/images/dot_clear.gif
/WEB-INF/web.xml
/WEB-INF/lib/editBean.jar
/WEB-INF/classes/com/javadesktop/servlets/viewServlet.class
/WEB-INF/classes/com/javadesktop/util/MyConversion.class
```

WEB.XML: THE DEPLOYMENT DESCRIPTOR

The `web.xml` file, commonly known as the deployment descriptor, contains configuration and deployment information about the Web application. It can contain information about the application in general, such as MIME type mappings, error pages, session configuration, and security. It can also contain information about definitions and mappings to both JSP pages and servlets. Another type of information that can be contained within the deployment descriptor is the servlet context initialization parameters.

ESSENTIAL NOTE: `WEB.XML` SECTION SEQUENCE

It is important to note that the DTD of the `web.xml` file defines a particular sequence in which entries can occur within the `web.xml` file.

Since many applications do not validate the XML of the `web.xml` file, an inappropriately set up `web.xml` file may be read without problems, but may not behave as expected. Worse still in these cases, the application will work until the required information from the `web.xml` file is needed.

Unfortunately, there are too many potential attributes to a `web.xml` file to list them all here. If the sequence of the sample `web.xml` file shown here is followed then it's fairly safe. Alternatively, finding out the exact details of the sequence would require examining the DTD itself.

Script 11.3 is a simple `web.xml` file created around a servlet and a JSP page. It includes a good selection of the different parameters that can be configured in a WAR file.

Script 11.3
A Simple `web.xml` Example

```
<!DOCTYPE web-app PUBLIC
    "-//Sun Microsystems, Inc.//DTD Web Application
    2.2//EN"
  "http://java.sun.com/j2ee/dtds/web-app_2_2.dtd">
<web-app>
  <display-name>Sample Application</display-name>
  <context-param>
    <param-name>email</param-name>
    <param-value>webmaster@javadesktop.com</param-value>
  </context-param>
  <servlet>
    <servlet-name></servlet-name>
```

```
      <description>no description</description>
      <jsp-file>index.jsp</jsp-file>
   </servlet>
   <servlet>
      <servlet-name>ViewData</servlet-name>
  <servlet-class>com.javadesktop.ViewData</servlet-class>
      <init-param>
        <param-name>Region</param-name>
        <param-value>North-East</param-value>
      </init-param>
   </servlet>
   <servlet-mapping>
      <servlet-name>ViewData</servlet-name>
      <url-pattern>/listing/*</url-pattern>
   </servlet-mapping>
   <session-config>
      <session-timeout>15</session-timeout>
   </session-config>
   <taglib>
      <taglib-uri>/taglib/mailtags</taglib-uri>
      <taglib-location>jsp/mailtags.tld</taglib-location>
   </taglib>
   <mime-mapping>
      <extension>pdf</extension>
      <mime-type>application/pdf</mime-type>
   </mime-mapping>
   <welcome-file-list>
      <welcome-file>index.jsp</welcome-file>
      <welcome-file>index.html</welcome-file>
      <welcome-file>main.htm</welcome-file>
   <welcome-file-list>
   <error-page>
      <error-code>404</error-code>
      <location>/error.html</location>
   </error-page>
</web-app>
```

As the deployment descriptor is an XML file, the first section is the DTD:

```
<!DOCTYPE web-app PUBLIC "-//Sun Microsystems, Inc.//DTD Web
      Application 2.2//EN"
"http://java.sun.com/j2ee/dtds/web-app_2_2.dtd">
```

Next, the `<web-app>` tag opens the definition of the Web application. The first entry within the `<web-app>` is the `<display-name>` tag, which represents a name for this particular Web application for GUI tools.

Next comes the parameters for the servlet context of this Web application:

```
<context-param>
  <param-name>email</param-name>
  <param-value>webmaster@javadesktop.com</param-value>
</context-param>
```

Here, a parameter with the name "`email`" is given a value of "`webmaster@javadesktop.com`". As all files in this Web application share the same servlet context, this parameter will be available to any JSP page or servlet contained within.

Following the servlet context parameters are the servlet definitions:

```
<servlet>
  <servlet-name></servlet-name>
  <jsp-file>index.jsp</jsp-file>
</servlet>
<servlet>
  <servlet-name>ViewData</servlet-name>
<servlet-class>com.javadesktop.ViewData</servlet-class>
  <init-param>
    <param-name>Region</param-name>
    <param-value>North-East</param-value>
  </init-param>
</servlet>
```

There are two servlet definitions here, one being a JSP page and one being a traditional servlet. `<servlet-name>` is the canonical name of the servlet, and is referenced in other sections of the `web.xml` file. JSP pages do not require a `<servlet-name>` tag. `<jsp-file>` contains the full path to a JSP file within the Web application. `<servlet-class>` describes the fully qualified class name of the servlet. Again, this is not necessary for JSP pages. `<init-param>` is used to describe parameters in name/value pairs similarly to the `<context-param>` tag. In this case, a parameter with the name "`Region`" is given a value of "`North-East`".

The next section of the deployment descriptor describes servlet mappings and is contained within `<servlet-mapping>` tags.

```
<servlet-mapping>
  <servlet-name>ViewData</servlet-name>
  <url-pattern>/listing/*</url-pattern>
</servlet-mapping>
```

Every servlet must be mapped to a URL pattern on the Web server. Notice that there is a `<servlet-name>` parameter tag here that corresponds to a servlet defined above in the `web.xml` file. The other tag contained within this section is the `<url-`

`pattern>` tag, which signifies the URL pattern with which to map the servlet. Also note that JSP pages do not require servlet mapping.

Next comes the `session` configuration section:

```
<session-config>
  <session-timeout>15</session-timeout>
</session-config>
```

The `<session-config>` section currently contains only one element: `<session-timeout>`. This element describes the default number of whole minutes that should pass before a session times out. This setting is for the whole Web application.

Next comes the `taglib` configuration section:

```
<taglib>
  <taglib-uri>/taglib/mailtags</taglib-uri>
  <taglib-location>jsp/mailtags.tld</taglib-location>
</taglib>
```

The `<taglib>` section defines how the application should register tag libraries. This essentially creates an alias from the given URI into the TLD. When the engine reads a reference to the URI within a `taglib` directive tag, it is able to match it to the corresponding location.

The `<taglib>` section is followed by the `<mime-mapping>` section:

```
<mime-mapping>
    <extension>pdf</extension>
    <mime-type>application/pdf</mime-type>
  </mime-mapping>
```

The `<mime-mapping>` section defines mappings between file extensions and MIME types. In this example, the Adobe Acrobat `pdf` file type is defined. After the MIME type section is the Welcome page section:

```
<welcome-file-list>
  <welcome-file>index.jsp</welcome-file>
  <welcome-file>index.html</welcome-file>
  <welcome-file>main.htm</welcome-file>
<welcome-file-list>
```

The Welcome page section defines an ordered list of filenames to use for the default file in a directory URL. In this example there are three file types listed to be selected. The final section in Script 11.3 is an <error-page> section:

```
<error-page>
  <error-code>404</error-code>
  <location>/error.html</location>
</error-page>
```

This section contains a mapping between an error code or exception type to the path of a resource in the Web application. In this example, the HTTP error code of 404 (File Not Found) is mapped to the URL /error.html.

In closing the Web application, there is a </web-app> tag. While Script 11.3 has a fair number of example tags used, deployment descriptors can be far more complex. For a detailed guide on the syntax of the web.xml file, see the Java Servlet 2.2 specification, available at the Sun Java Web site: *http://www.java.sun.com/*.

While an understanding of the capabilities and syntax of the web.xml file is important, WAR files and web.xml files can be quickly created and edited utilizing the Application Deployment Tool that is packaged with the J2EE development kit. This tool is commonly known as DeployTool.

11.2.3 Sun DeployTool

The Sun Application Deployment Tool, or DeployTool, is an excellent cross-platform means of creating EAR, WAR, and JAR files. It is distributed with the J2EE SDK, which is available from Sun Microsystems without cost. It is distributed on Microsoft Windows and Sun Sparc platforms, but should be able to run on any Java 2 JVM.

To utilize the DeployTool to create WAR, JAR, and EAR files, the application must first be installed. It is packaged with the J2EE SDK, and can be downloaded from the Sun Java Web site (*http://www.java.sun.com/*). Once installed, be sure that environmental variables for JAVA_HOME and J2EE_HOME are set. Next, DeployTool can be launched by executing the appropriate script for your system (usually deploytool.bat or deploytool.sh). Once launched, DeployTool should display a screen similar to that of Figure 11–5.

DeployTool is an EAR file-centric application, so before a WAR file can be created, a new application object must be created. To do this, choose "New Application . . ." from the "File" menu. If a WAR file is desired, the name of the application is unimportant.

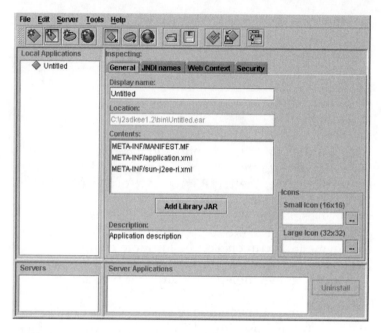

FIGURE 11–5 DeployTool Primary Interface

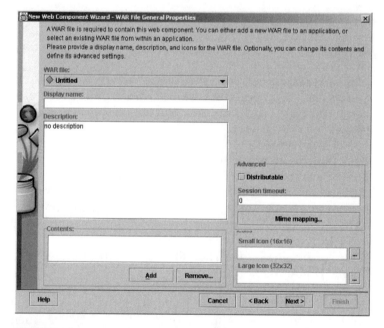

FIGURE 11–6 DeployTool WAR File Component Interface

Next, a new Web application needs to be created. To do this, select "New Web Component..." from the "File" menu. This starts the WAR file wizard. After an informational screen, the wizard should look like Figure 11–6. This screen is used to configure information that pertains to the entire WAR application.

This page is used to add contents to the WAR file. To do this, click on the "Add..." button. A screen comes up looking like Figure 11–7.

This is the first of two screens that allows files to be added to the WAR file. This first screen is for Java class files, including JAR files. In this section, all servlets, JavaBeans, and other utility class files should be added. When complete, the "Next" button should be selected. This brings up a similar page, this time for content files. The page should look like Figure 11–8. Content files include HTML pages, XML pages, image files, style sheets, and other Web-based components, as well as JSP pages.

After clicking "Next," a screen comes up asking whether the Web component will contain a servlet, JSP page, or no Web component. Select the correct choice, and then choose "Finish." While

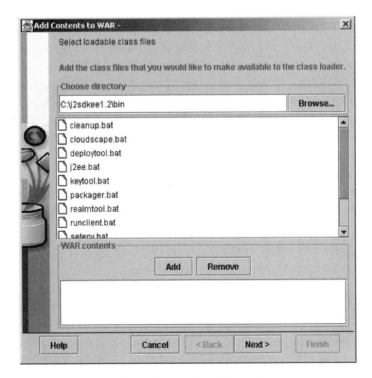

FIGURE 11–7 DeployTool Add Class File Interface

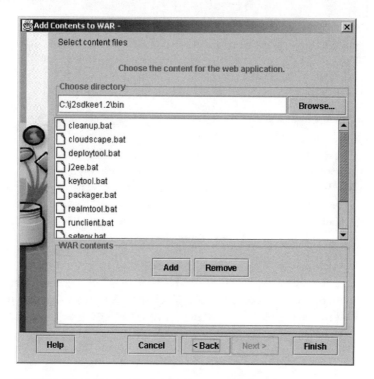

FIGURE 11–8 DeployTool Add Content File Interface

there are other configuration options, this is the default number of choices necessary to create a WAR file.

DeployTool should now be back at the original opening page. To save the WAR file, select the "Web App" object in the "Local Applications" tree hierarchy. Then, choose "Save As . . ." from the "File" menu. While this was only a quick run-through of DeployTool's capabilities, it should be obvious that it is a time-saving tool for creating WAR files.

◆ 11.3 Recap

While the design and deployment options for JSP programs are somewhat new, they contain enterprise-class strategies for architecting and releasing applications. As there are several different options to choose from, the JSP author soon realizes that there is more than one way to create an application. The key is to use the versatility and options of JSP design and deployment to develop an application that best suits the production environment's needs and requirements.

12 The Future of JSP

It is obvious that JSP development has a large future in Web application development. It is almost weekly that a new or existing application is released with JSP support. This is testament to the flexibility of JSP.

It is also important to note that JSP is a fairly new specification, so keep sharp eyes out for new specifications and enhancements.

◆ 12.1 The Impact of J2EE

With the release of J2EE, a new world of standards-based Web applications has emerged. Developers of Web application servers are scrambling to write J2EE compliance into their servers. Java developers are excited about the ability to package and deploy their applications in a common format that can be transferred across servers and platforms.

Never before have EJB, DCOM, and CORBA applications been so easy to integrate. J2EE provides the foundation for every part of designing, developing, and deploying Web applications.

With the widespread adoption of J2EE comes the integration of JSP. JSP provides the front-end for enterprise Java applications on the Web, and plays a vital role in developing scalable, cross-platform software. As Web applications become more sophisticated, the capabilities of JSP will grow.

◆ 12.2 JSP and GUI Tools

As the popularity of JSP increases, look for the integration of JSP page creation in HTML page development tools to increase. JSP was built from the ground up to be easy to parse, thus making it easily editable in a development tool.

Already many popular environments such as Macromedia Dreamweaver, Adobe GoLive, and Allaire Homesite have announced JSP integration. These are just the forefront of a wave of JSP/HTML tools to hit the market.

Also look for Java IDEs to feature JSP integration and debugging. Sun's Forte for Java and IBM WebSphere Studio already feature these tools, and many of their competitors have announced future integration.

By far, the most promising part of JSP is the concept of tag libraries, which are ripe for integration into both JSP/HTML editors as well as Java IDEs. With their portable framework, XML syntax, and advanced configuration features, they are perfect for packaging and deploying reusable JSP components.

In the future, different development environments with JSP support will share components in the form of tag libraries. With their ability to hide underlying logic, they are perfect for software developers who want to develop tools that protect intellectual property while giving maximum flexibility.

All in all, JSP pages will play an important role in development environments. They allow for quick creation and deployment of Web applications, which is important in today's mindset of Internet time.

◆ 12.3 XML, XML, and more XML

In the future, XML will also play a major role in Web application development. JSP pages are perfect for both XML page generation as well as integration into XML tools. This is mostly due to the close relationship JSP has with Java, as well as the fact that Java hosts a comprehensive set of XML tools and libraries. The large set of tools available for manipulating XML is key here, as these tools can also be used to manipulate XML pages that are written to be XML-compliant.

While it is probably not true that XML will eventually replace HTML, it is probably true that HTML will become fully XML-compliant. In addition, XML is playing an ever-increasing role in applications beyond the Web. From application integration, to configuration management, to standardization, XML will play an important role in the future of enterprise applications.

While JSP is well integrated into XML, the JSP specification authors promise to add further integration in future releases of JSP. This is due to the integration of XML tools into the standard JDKs. Be certain that the future of XML will play a vital role in the development of the JSP specification.

◆ 12.4 Where Do We Go from Here?

While JSP page applications are excellent tools on their own, they are only the tip of the iceberg for most enterprise Web applications. They are the icing on the cake, so to speak. They represent the final step of an application before data is presented to the user. Once JSP is mastered, a software developer should move the focus to the back office, learning the underlying core applications.

Relational and object-oriented database management systems are a good place to start, as they form the foundation for most Web applications. The next step would be to learn one or more of the distributed component environments, such as EJB, CORBA, or DCOM.

Another good area of study is enterprise application integration (EAI). For the most part, the data needed in applications is out there, often in legacy or disparate systems. Connecting those systems to share data is often the biggest challenge.

Whatever area of study and development a developer chooses to follow, the techniques and models learned from JSP development serve as a solid stepping-stone for keeping pace with the rapid evolution of today's software development.

Index

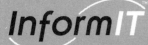